The
NEW JERSEY
FOOD TRUCK
Cookbook

PATRICK LOMBARDI AND VINCENT PARISI
OF BESTOFNJ.COM

AMERICAN PALATE

Published by American Palate
A Division of The History Press
Charleston, SC
www.historypress.com

First published 2023

Manufactured in the United States

ISBN 9781467151771

Library of Congress Control Number: 2022947156

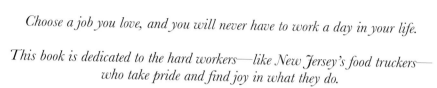

Choose a job you love, and you will never have to work a day in your life.

This book is dedicated to the hard workers—like New Jersey's food truckers—who take pride and find joy in what they do.

CONTENTS

Contents

SHOWCASING NEW JERSEY FOOD TRUCKS

The idea to develop a series centered on New Jersey food trucks came on Friday, December 29, 2017, at 12:07 p.m. Patrick Lombardi, photographer and longtime writer for BestofNJ.com, was working on an assignment interviewing the owners of Bearded One BBQ for a standalone feature on our website. While transcribing the interview, Patrick noted the owners were quick to mention—completely unprovoked—the deep bonds and close relationships they had formed with the other food truckers who attended the same events. So Patrick got to thinking.

Patrick sent me an email, mentioning, "It might make a pretty cool series to showcase a different New Jersey food truck every month/every other week or so." As the editor-in-chief for Best of NJ, I like to be collaborative with our writing team. While much of their work comes from assignments they receive from me, I have an open-pitch policy for both new stories and potential series. Patrick had been mulling over the idea for a food truck series for a while, so by the time he sent me his pitch idea, it was a pretty fleshed-out concept.

"The articles could have a little background on the food trucks, a transcribed interview and nice photos of what treats they offer," he described. I knew right away the idea was worth pursuing. Seven minutes later, at 12:14 p.m., I responded, giving him the green light to get started. "I like the idea. Maybe as a limited series we release each year from spring–summer during the bulk of food truck festivals. Let me know which food truck vendors you're thinking about including. But overall, yeah, I think we can give this a shot," I said.

We launched the series—simply titled "The Best New Jersey Food Trucks"—on March 30, 2018, featuring who else but Bearded One BBQ in our inaugural publication. The response from readers and other food truckers was immediate. They loved the idea and wanted to see more of their favorite trucks—and the people behind them—featured on Best of NJ. The series moved ahead as planned, as a limited series focusing on six food trucks per year from March through August. By the end of that first year, we had interest from enough food truck owners—plus nominations from readers—to keep the series going for years to come.

Since the series debut, we've been fortunate enough to profile twenty-seven food trucks (at the time of writing this preface) and counting. While some of them may have slightly similar food menus, they all have unique stories to tell. We've met food truck owners who have rebounded from bankruptcy, award-winning chefs who have no formal cooking training at all and even a food truck that literally fell off a cliff (well, twenty feet down off Henry Hudson Drive in Fort Lee, anyway). The point is, there's a near infinite well of amazing stories to tell from New Jersey's food truck community.

After a few years of releasing our online series, I wanted to pursue a traditional publishing route. Nothing on the internet lasts forever, and I wanted a way to immortalize some of the amazing stories and people we've met in the years since "The Best New Jersey Food Trucks" debuted. I originally intended to produce an oversized coffee table book featuring large color photos of the trucks, the teams behind them and their signature menu items. But I learned from a number of potential publishers that coffee table books are expensive to produce, which results in higher purchase prices for readers, and that wasn't the best option for this first book. Surprisingly, it took only a few months before one of the publishers I reached out to expressed interest, and soon we had a clear path to publication.

I hope readers enjoy trying the included recipes at home and that it inspires them to attend more food truck festivals and other events where food trucks are present. I hope it encourages readers to chat with the food truck owners—without holding up the line!—and ask about how they ended up starting a food truck, because I guarantee there's an interesting story there. But most importantly, I hope it inspires readers to try some delicious new foods they may otherwise have walked right past, whether it's cheesecake on a stick, a brisket grilled cheese sandwich or a BLT lobster roll.

—Vincent Parisi

ACKNOWLEDGEMENTS

There's no community like the food truck community. The industry is often glamorized on television and in movies, made to appear like some lax service business with low overhead and little work. The amount of effort and drive (pun intended) it takes to run, maintain and operate a food truck is no joke, and the ones who last wouldn't be out there if they didn't truly love what they do—blood, sweat, tears and all.

When I first started going to food truck festivals, I had no idea what went into the business. I figured it was easy enough to finance a truck, stock some food and supplies, post up on any busy city street and make buckets of cash every day. (Sometimes I still laugh at my foolishness.) I had no idea about commissary kitchens—or permits, health and fire inspections, county and township fees, event charges, street vending statutes, food and supply shortages, water reserve, five-thousand-watt generators, outfitting commercial vehicles, employing staff, scheduling events, developing a menu and scrupulous inventorying. Not to mention, it takes me twenty minutes to microwave taquitos—foodies don't have that kind of time.

If you're ever wondering how difficult it might be to run a food truck, just think about how painstaking it is to keep up with car maintenance. Now imagine you have a kitchen in your backseat, and every time you park, four different people have their hands out looking for payment. Then, after driving fifty miles away from your home, someone comes up to your window just to complain that you're charging too much for fries.

It's not all bad. It truly isn't. But all of these challenges underscore just how outstanding the owners in this book—and other food truck operators—are, in that they juggle all of that and more and still deliver quality food. And if it weren't for these struggles, the food truck community wouldn't be as strong as it is today. The owners and workers have built bonds since seeing each other day in and day out. More so, however, they're there for each other whenever someone runs out of serving boats or someone else's generator dies. They hang out, joke around and share their stories, laughs and, of course, food.

So I owe much more than a debt of gratitude to every single one of the food truck owners in this book. All of you have allowed me to step into your trucks, restaurants and kitchens; you've let me sample your food, take myriad photos and ask you insufferably endless questions. And most of you still pretend to be happy when you see me! So I appreciate your patience and constant assistance.

A big thank-you to the D'Addario, Miller, Fahnholz and Bzdewka families for your time and cooperation in showcasing such esteemed family businesses. Janet, Gene Jr. and Jeff Maddalena and Matt Miller and Scott Bevis—you're a resilient team, and thank you for letting me into your shop and kitchen many times, even though I know you're crazy busy. Dean and Emily Hodecker, Lai and Gustavo Barboni, Henry Sanchez and Brenda Rosa, Karen Pabon and Rockeem Magbie, Desiree and Paul Bagnell and Dan and Russel Hover—you all are brilliantly hardworking "power couples," and your dedication to your businesses and your life partners is inspirational.

Thank you also to Andrew Dudich, Kiersten Connor, Fumiji Aoki, Cindy Matas and Jonathan Anderson, who all are exceptional and inspirational independent owners who have dedicated a lot of their time to helping with this book. John Fels and Bobby O'Donnell, Eduardo Rojas and Alex Sanchez, Carlos Castillo along with Fernando Campo and Martín Moliné, and James and Dana Costello along with Candy Blake, Gavin DeCapua and Matthew Smith—your partnerships are invaluable, and that shows through the wonderful work you do every day with your food trucks and restaurants. It has been a privilege to get to know you all. Thank you for allowing me to tell your stories and share your food with countless other New Jersey foodies like us.

Thank you to BestofNJ.com and editor-in-chief Vinny Parisi for this opportunity and for allowing me to write for their super cool site for so many years. It has always been a joy.

I also want to thank my own family, who didn't check me into a hospital when I expressed that I wanted to become a writer. Your constant support and interest in my work—including your active interest in food trucks—is what kept me an avid reader and a passionate writer.

Finally, I couldn't have possibly finished this book, done the series or really published anything without the unyielding support from my wife, Christine. She's been an extension of this project since the very beginning, accompanying me to countless events, sitting in on the interviews, listening to me moan and lament whenever I'd accidentally erase an article draft or folder of photographs. (You read that right—it happened *more than once*.) She has encouraged and endured me throughout every step of my writing career and has kept me going when I wanted to give it up. Thank you, Christine.

—Patrick Lombardi

~~~

Thank you to the New Jersey food truck community for allowing us into your space—oftentimes literally—and to tell your stories. I am humbled by and grateful for your willingness to share your personal adventures, your delicious recipes and your time. I hope this book captures at least a sliver of the uniqueness New Jersey's food trucking scene has to offer and capably showcases the wonderful people behind some of the state's best mobile cuisine.

I also want to thank BestofNJ.com's loyal readers for making this possible in the first place. When Patrick and I first developed our original web series, "The Best New Jersey Food Trucks," back in 2018, I don't think either of us realized just how popular food trucks would become. It's an absolute pleasure to be able to introduce these incredible food trucks, and the people behind them, to our readers both online and, now, in print as well. I know I speak for both of us when I say we look forward to meeting many more food truckers—and sampling their tasty menus—for many years to come.

A special thank-you to my wife and best friend, Kristen. It's no secret that I'm a workaholic in a demanding job that is easy to disappear into; I will forever appreciate all the late nights you allow me to spend sitting at my laptop when I should really be sitting next to you on the couch. Your patience, support and understanding make it possible for me to do the ceaseless, important work I do supporting local businesses. Our growing family—which will have expanded significantly by the time this book hits store shelves, thanks to the recent news that we are expecting twin boys— is what keeps me motivated to grow as a person, a husband and a leader at work, and I hope to constantly improve at all three (not to mention the additional, impending role of father to my sons, Adam and Oliver).

Finally, thank you to my family for allowing me the freedom to pursue the unpredictable career choice that is online publishing. Going all-in on a simple premise like "promoting things to do in New Jersey" seems like a much more haphazard and irresponsible decision in hindsight, but it turned out to be the best job I could ever dream of. If any work worth doing requires effort, pain and difficulty, I'm definitely on the right path.

—Vincent Parisi

ADDICTED TO FOOD (TRUCKS)

Not one of the trucks in this book has ever served me a meal that *didn't* make me lick the wax-paper boat when I was done. At food truck festivals across New Jersey, you'll probably find me nose deep in a taco bowl or brisket grilled cheese's foil wrap. Either that or I'm picking at the crumbs of a fried buffalo chicken egg roll or fresh Cuban sandwich. Sure, I could always go order a second helping—which I do—but I still crave every last morsel. I'm not embarrassed by it.

One might say I love food trucks a little *too* much. My wife and I even had one (Good Food = Good Mood) cater our pandemic wedding in my mother-in-law's backyard. But that's reductive of the relationship New Jersey has developed with food trucks in recent years. Point being: I'm not nearly the only one who loves them.

Food trucks have become a booming industry in the Garden State, each one a powerhouse of culinary innovation—on *wheels*. Those greasy lunch trucks that serve industrial parks and college campuses after 2:00 a.m.—well, they're still around and admittedly a guilty pleasure. But they didn't just slap on a GOURMET sticker and start catering bridal showers. No, this generation of food trucks is a whole new fleet. They'll burn past you on the parkway and then hand you a heaping pile of pulled pork fries with a smile. They're a family on the road who always have each other's backs in the fields. Some will pound the pavement as early as 6:00 a.m. and won't get back home until midnight. They don't waste time worrying about "competition" because each truck offers something different. We as foodies make room in our stomachs for a taste of every last one of them, anyway.

The best of them don't just throw patties on a flat top and drench their buns in butter; they spend most of their weeks prepping and cooking in commissary kitchens, scrutinizing each ingredient and every step. They've developed exclusive recipes and precise methods that can't be pumped out of an assembly line. When they're not cooking, they are on their hands and knees scrubbing every inch of their mobile kitchen. No corners are cut and no avenues ignored.

You'll find many of those mouthwatering recipes in this book, which features twenty of the best food trucks from all around the state. Thanks to the masterminds who have already perfected their signature dishes, you'll learn how to cook like an elite New Jersey food trucker. Each truck has a distinct cuisine, teaching you how to make everything from Surf N Turf Burger Sliders to Chookie desserts (which is a cheesecake sandwiched between two chocolate chip cookies). Despite their differences in menu, each truck shares a common thread: they all cook with *respect* for both their patrons and their products, serving meals that leave you smooching the plate it was served on. After trying a few recipes on your own, you won't be embarrassed about doing it, either.

—Patrick Lombardi

PART I

....

NORTH JERSEY FOOD TRUCKS

....

1. Carlitos Barbecue Taqueria
Recipe: Crispy Lechon
Biography
Q&A with Founder Carlos Castillo

2. Chick Wings & Things
Recipe: Romesco Sauce
Biography
Q&A with Owners Karen Pabon and Rockeem Magbie

3. Cubano X-Press
Recipe: Tofu Picadillo
Recipe: Latin-Style Rice Pilaf with Black Beans
Biography
Q&A with Owners Henry Sanchez and Brenda Rosa

4. Ms. Fu's Yummy Food Truck
Recipe: Lettuce Wrap
Recipe: Yakisoba Noodles
Biography
Q&A with Owner Fumiji Aoki

5. The Brownie Bar
Recipe: Massimo's (non)Gingerbread Cookies
Biography
Q&A with Co-Founder Lai Barboni

CHAPTER 1

CARLITOS BARBECUE TAQUERIA

Crispy Lechon (Pork Shoulder)

Half an onion
2 tomatoes
3 oranges (for juice)
4 limes (for juice)
6 cloves garlic
2 pinches cilantro
2 tablespoons fresh oregano
1 (7- to-8 pound) pork shoulder/butt
4 ounces olive oil
2 ounces kosher salt
2 ounces Sazon seasoning

Prep: To make marinade, combine half onion, tomatoes, orange juice, lime juice, garlic cloves, cilantro and oregano in a blender. Blend until a viscous liquid.

Skin side down, stab fifteen to twenty slits into the meaty part of the pork shoulder. Then flip back over so that the skin side is facing up and place in large bowl.

Pour marinade over pork shoulder. Cover and place in refrigerator for 24 to 48 hours.

Remove pork shoulder from bowl and dry.

Cooking: Preheat oven to 350 degrees Fahrenheit.

Coat pork shoulder with olive oil and rub into meat.

Season the pork shoulder first with salt, then with Sazon seasoning.

Place pork shoulder on roasting tray and put in oven. Cook for 6 hours.

Remove meat from oven and let rest for 10 minutes.

Meat should be tender, meaning you can tear it apart with your hands, removing cap first.

Chop up cap, then enjoy crispy lechon in a taco, slider or however you'd like.

~~~

From Backyard Barbecues to Statewide Success

Carlos Castillo grew up in Corona, Queens, New York. He and his family moved from Honduras to the United States in 1989 and were immediately immersed in the country's diverse culture and cuisine. From an early age, Carlos was ordering from food trucks and street vendors from around the world who settled in his New York City borough. It was a tradition he shared with his father since the early 1990s: the two would experience different cultures through the food just outside their doorway.

As an adult, Carlos hosted an annual backyard barbecue for up to fifty people. He always loved cooking, and this event was a way to hone his hobby. But Carlos wanted cooking to be more than a hobby; he wanted to open his own restaurant. Just to be certain, he started as a dishwasher at a distinguished eatery right on the Hudson River. He also went back to school and earned his bachelor's degree from the New York City College of Technology in Brooklyn.

A few months later, Carlos took a job at a major hospitality company called Sodexo US, where he met Fernando Campo, the general manager of the Swiss Airlines account at John F. Kennedy International Airport. They worked closely together, and when Fernando left a year later, Carlos took over as general manager.

LOVE AT FIRST BITE

In 2008, Carlos tried American barbecue for the first time. He was mesmerized by the smoky aroma, distinct textures and juicy meat. Of course, Carlos had other types of barbecue before, but this American style hit differently. There was no mistaking it. Carlos enjoyed every mouthful but

thought there was one thing missing: a tortilla. He spent the following years making his own barbecue: smoking his own brisket and pork, trying different types of wood, creating his own dry rubs and contemplating sauces.

Carlos moved to New Jersey in 2015. From the moment he settled into his home, he wanted to start a food truck. He told his now-wife, Sabrina, about the idea, and she was all in from the beginning. The pair worked on perfecting their barbecue, and once they were ready to showcase their products, Carlos knew the next partner he wanted to team up with: Fernando.

Fernando agreed immediately. The trio pooled their combined savings, and with some help from a successful Kickstarter campaign, they opened their food trailer.

A Humble Start

Carlitos started small. Carlos and Fernando purchased one trailer, providing enough room for both of them to prepare and serve the orders. They got it built out and wrapped with their logos and then finalized their menu. Carlitos took to the streets and debuted during lunch service at Exchange Place in Jersey City. They parked on the side of Grand Street, right in front of Goldman Sachs, and waited for the lunch rush. It was a modest turnout, but Carlos and Fernando considered their first foray into the food trucking world a success.

Carlitos spent much of the first year operating during Monday-through-Friday lunch services. Carlos considers the entirety of year one a learning experience and, most importantly, a chance to perfect their recipes.

Carlos's smoked meats have a distinct (delicious) flavor and tender bite. He doesn't mask the quality of his brisket with barbecue sauce. Instead, he pairs his tacos with any combination of cheeses, pickled onions, salsa and their own guacamole sauce. Tacos are also available with chicken, beef, carne asada, fish and pulled pork. The sweet plantain taco is a hearty serving for a vegetarian option. His side dishes include authentic Mexican street corn (grilled corn, Cotija cheese, mayonnaise and chili pepper).

Expanding the Brand

Initially, Carlos and Fernando continued their full-time jobs while operating Carlitos. But Carlos realized the only way the business could work was if he devoted all of his professional time to it. So Carlos left his full-time job to focus on Carlitos, and Fernando soon did the same.

The two struggled to stay afloat at first, but opportunities soon presented themselves. In 2018, Carlitos opened a brick-and-mortar restaurant inside the Westfield Garden State Plaza in Paramus. But since the food truck had already become a handful, Carlos and Fernando decided to recruit a third partner: Martín Moliné, a childhood friend with a background in finance.

After adding Martín to the team, the three partners were able to expand the business. Fernando is responsible for much of the operations, including hands-on work and planning. Meanwhile, Carlos focuses more on the creative side and the community engagement. Martín handles things on the administrative side and develops growth strategies for the business. Together, they've been able to take Carlitos from a lunch service trailer on the side of Grand Street and turn it into a layered barbecue business that serves both New Jersey and New York City.

Q&A WITH FOUNDER CARLOS CASTILLO

What came first, the restaurant or the truck?

The truck. Date of birth was July 17, 2017, in Jersey City. It was just lunch service. It was lunchtime start at Exchange Place in Jersey City. It was Fernando and myself. We parked on Grand Street right in front of Goldman Sachs. I think we saw about forty people, and we were so happy! I remember the first customer's name was Adam [laughs]. He worked at Goldman Sachs. And we were just so surprised and happy that people were paying for our food. You feel like you made it that day. People actually were willing to come up to our window and buy our food.

How has the truck evolved over the years since then?

Year one was a lot of Monday through Friday, getting to understand our operation. Barbecue itself is about mastering and perfecting your recipes. So the truck basically gave us some sort of continuity and allowed us to standardize our recipes. Then it was about connecting with people there and seeing who's willing to buy into this concept. And then we evolved.

Fernando and I were still working full-time jobs, but once we quit our jobs to go into this full time, we had to make this work in a different way. We had to generate more income. So we started doing dinner service mostly at luxury condominium buildings where there's high population. So we did

some of that for a while. Now, we utilize our trailer mostly for large-scale events. We'll attend large events, festivals and street markets and fairs with our truck.

You once talked about the first time you had barbecue and wanted a tortilla to go along with it. Talk about that idea and its role in developing Carlitos.

It was interesting to me; growing up in Queens, there wasn't a lot of barbecue in our neighborhood. It just was not a popular thing there, or it just wasn't prominent. So as a kid, that wasn't something I grew up eating. I didn't have that kind of access. So the first time I had barbecue was a very special day. But I was just so used to eating with a tortilla, so I said, "I have to make this happen."

I tried experimenting and exploring with different types of barbecue, different tortillas and different items. I knew this definitely had legs and continued with the research and development, self-taught myself barbecue, learned the tortilla-making process from scratch and combined my favorite foods.

What items are on the Carlitos menu?

It's a small menu. We focus on quality, sourcing quality ingredients and a lot of precision. We sell barbecue tacos. I think any barbecue person will tell you that you really get graded on the quality of your brisket. It's the hardest thing to make in the barbecue world, at least from what I've experienced. So we started with perfecting the brisket, at least to our liking and to the taco experience. We wanted to create a very moist and flavorful, smoky brisket. Our menu's basically inspired by barbecue culture and Mexican culture. Essentially, our proteins are the barbecue element. We stay away from barbecue sauce because we don't want to hide the quality of the meat.

Our main items are tacos, and we offer three different tacos. We have the brisket, pulled pork and chicken. There's also a vegetarian taco with seared cheese and sweet plantains on a tortilla. That one has a cult following, and it took the longest to develop, because we focus so much on our meats.

We also have other things like Mexican street corn, which is very traditional. We also offer basics like guac and chips. We do all in-house pickling, and all our salsas are made from scratch. We also sell a rice bowl with cilantro lime rice, choice of meat and sweet plantains.

Do you offer catering?

We provide three different experiences. We have a package for smaller parties or for offices. For office settings, we do a minimum of fifty people. We offer pickup for smaller parties, but if we come to you, we ask that the party size be at least fifty people.

For the second package, we get a lot of phone calls about the trailer. So we offer that as well. The entire menu with all the truck fees and stuff is available online.

Then we have the *carrito*, which is a taco cart. It's pretty much self-sufficient; we just need electricity. You can either be indoors or outdoors. It's a really cool way to celebrate quinceañeras or sweet sixteens, bar mitzvahs, all that stuff. The nice thing about the carrito is the tortilla pressing happens right in front of you, so you get to see that whole thing. We sear the cheese in front of you, so you get to experience all that. You get to see it fresh, and you're getting it right off the grill, and that's the best time to have a taco. Fresh, hot tortilla, hot meat—you can eat it right away, and that's the best.

CHAPTER 2
CHICK WINGS & THINGS

Romesco Sauce

¼ cup olive oil
5 garlic cloves, minced
I whole roasted red pepper
5 whole plum tomatoes, freshly peeled or from can
¼ cup parsley, dried or freshly chopped
½ lemon
Salt, to taste

Heat olive oil in pan on medium-high heat for 2 minutes.

Add minced garlic, roasted red pepper and plum tomatoes, and stir.

While mixing, add parsley, then squeeze in lemon juice. Add salt to taste.

Pour from pan to bowl or container and let rest for 10 minutes.

Use as dipping sauce or toss with chicken wings.

Optional: add your favorite hot peppers for heat.

IT'S A CHICK WING THING

Chick Wings & Things might seem unassuming at first. The depictions of wings, sliders and fries above the window look too good to be real. A rooster and hen adorn the side of the trailer above their slogan: "Pretty Fly for Wing Guys." The bright colors are eye-catching, but is it all for show?

Not even a little bit.

Owners Karen Pabon and Rockeem Magbie know chicken. They care about their food, putting years of experience to work when scrutinizing each element of their menu. From meat to buns to sides, the couple looks for the best ingredients and products so that guests get unparalleled wings and things—a notion that's clear from the very first bite.

The Chick Wings & Things journey was nearly two decades in the making. Karen and Rockeem first met in New York City in 2004. Karen was born and raised in Glasgow, Scotland, coming from a large family with eight brothers and three sisters. She always had a dream of visiting the United States of America, with her eyes set on the illustrious New York City. As much as she loved Scotland, she wanted to try something different. In 1993, that dream became a reality when she moved to the Empire State. Her plan was to work as a nanny for a while before heading back to Scotland. But it wasn't long before Karen decided to stay; and although she's visited her home country over the past three decades, her life is now in America.

Meanwhile, Rockeem grew up in New York. After high school, he started studying computer science but soon lost interest and pivoted career paths. Living in the Lower East Side of Manhattan, Rockeem eventually began driving buses and working for the post office. All the while, his goal was to open his own business, something he could put his name on and be creative with.

INCUBATING AN IDEA

About a year into their relationship, Karen and Rockeem moved to New Jersey. They decided to start their own business, with Karen hoping for a brick-and-mortar and Rockeem pushing for a food truck. Their first business together was called K&R Hamburgers & Hotdogs. Despite Karen and Rockeem's lack of formal culinary training, they made an excellent team and had a strong passion for delivering quality food.

K&R Hamburgers & Hotdogs featured a massive menu. The business sold, of course, hamburgers and hot dogs, but guests could also order cheesesteaks, breakfast items and even gyros. Although the feedback was tremendous, the food costs were daunting, and the couple knew they had to make a change. Just four years after starting their first business, Karen and Rockeem rebranded as Chick Wings & Things, narrowing their menu to the fan-favorite items they offer today.

With their second venture underway, Karen and Rockeem sought to reinvent their model. Chicken wings were an obvious choice when planning their menu and brand. Friends and family would ask Karen and Rockeem to cook wings every year for their Super Bowl parties and other occasions— they were better than any restaurant or caterer around.

But the food truck also offers non-chicken options, like mozzarella sticks, onion rings and waffle fries. The most popular items, however, are the wings (obviously), chicken sliders, tenders and pulled chicken. Their poultry dishes are always tender and juicy, but everything on the menu is consistent in quality, including the jumbo, meaty wings fried fresh to order.

However, no wing is complete without dipping sauce, and Chick Wings & Things does not disappoint. They offer traditional flavors like buffalo and barbecue, but fans know the real winners are the specialty sauces. These not-so-secret sauces include Spicy Orange and Garlic Parmesan. For 2022, the

Chicken wings with Romesco sauce in a basket, along with Romesco sauce ingredients.

couple introduced a Romesco sauce to the menu. This mild, tomato-based sauce pairs nicely with chicken, fish and even beef.

Karen and Rockeem show no signs of slowing down. Despite focusing on a more condensed menu than their initial idea, the duo is always experimenting with and serving new ideas and top-quality dishes. Chick Wings & Things is a staple at food truck events across the state and is also consistently busy catering parties or providing lunch for first responders and hospital workers. Walking up to the truck, you'll always find Karen behind the counter and Rockeem behind the fryer, putting smiles on the faces of each and every patron.

Q&A with Owners Karen Pabon and Rockeem Magbie

How would you describe Chick Wings & Things?

Karen: I don't want to say that we're unique, but no one else really does wings.

Rockeem: Yeah, when we started, I think there was only one other wing truck, and it was in the city.

Karen: Rockeem makes all of the sauces homemade.

Rockeem: And we try to stick to our chicken theme; everything has chicken. So everyone knows what they're going to get when they come to us—they're going to get chicken [laughs].

What sets you apart from other trucks?

Rockeem: I think, honestly, it's the sauces. Like we said, they're all homemade sauces. We put a lot of thought—and love [laughs]—into our sauces, and I hope it shows. And I think another key to our success is our speed. We try to get everything out as quickly as possible, under a minute, if possible. Pacing—that's the key.

Do you always offer the same wing sauces, or are there some seasonal flavors?

Rockeem: We always offer the same sauces on our truck. We have Buffalo, Citrus Barbecue, Garlic Parmesan, Garlic Lemon Pepper, Teriyaki and Spicy Orange.

Karen: I'd say Garlic Parmesan and Buffalo are the two most popular sauces. We always get so many orders for those at events.

What are your most popular non-wing menu items?

Rockeem: I would say our pulled chicken sliders. That's a big hit. Also, people love the homemade chili; they love when they dig into the fries and get that extra meat. Their expressions are the best when they see the presentation.

What sort of catering options do you offer?

Karen: We really enjoy catering. We'll do any type of event: graduation parties, weddings, anniversaries, corporate events, Super Bowl parties, anything.

Rockeem: You name it, we'll be there.

Karen: And we'll travel far. We've gone down to Wildwood and even up to Connecticut. And everything we offer on the truck is available for catering events.

CHAPTER 3

CUBANO X-PRESS

Tofu Picadillo

½ cup olive oil
10 sliced olives
1 bunch scallions
3 cloves garlic
5 tomatoes, diced
2 medium red peppers
1 small bunch cilantro, chopped
2 small cans Goya tomato sauce
1 tablespoon cumin
1 packet Sazon seasoning
1 teaspoon soy sauce
Salt, to taste
Pepper, to taste
2 (1-pound) squares of extra firm tofu

Tofu Picadillo: In a medium pot over high heat, sauté olive oil, olives, scallions, garlic, diced tomatoes, red peppers and cilantro. Sauté until aroma starts to come out of mixture in pot.

Add tomato sauce and let simmer for 10 minutes.

Season with cumin, Sazon and soy sauce. This will become your sofrito.

Cut tofu to desired size squares (½ inch to an inch), add to sofrito and serve.

About Sofrito: This is a Latin mother sauce. I use it as my flavor base for several dishes. I add it to paella, beans, ropa vieja, chicken fricassee and so much more. Its flavor is so powerful. It definitely is something to always have handy. Can also be store-bought sofrito, red or green, by Goya.

—Henry Sanchez

Latin-Style Rice Pilaf with Black Beans

Latin-Style Rice Pilaf (Yield: 4 servings)
2 cups rice
3 cups water
1 tablespoon salt
1 tablespoon butter
1 bay leaf
2 tablespoons olive oil

Black Beans (Yield: 4 servings)
1 pound dry black beans
6 ounces sofrito (see Tofu Picadillo recipe)
2 packets Sazon seasoning
1 tablespoon cumin
1 teaspoon salt
1 teaspoon pepper

Latin-Style Rice Pilaf: Preheat oven to 375 degrees Fahrenheit. Mix all ingredients together in stainless-steel pan and cover with aluminum foil. Bake for 45 minutes. Remove from oven and serve while warm.

Black Beans: Soak beans in water overnight. Cook beans in boiling water for about 1 hour, or until beans are tender. When done, add all ingredients and bring to a boil. Then let simmer for 10 minutes.

Combine: Strain beans and serve atop Latin-Style Rice Pilaf.

~~~

A Road Well Traveled

Henry Sanchez was born and raised in New Jersey. His love of cooking eventually took him out of the state—but also brought him right back. He and his partner, Brenda Rosa, developed Cubano X-Press, a mobile eatery honoring their backgrounds, passions and experiences.

Henry has been working in kitchens since he was sixteen years old. After graduating high school, he enrolled at the Culinary Institute of America in Hyde Park, New York. He desired to experience all different types of cuisine, as well as the diverse culinary industry outside New Jersey. He spent the early years of his career working in several prestigious positions in Manhattan, including as executive chef of Gallaghers Steakhouse on 52nd Street. From there, Henry traveled down to Miami, Florida, expanding his knowledge and appreciation of Caribbean food. After four years, Henry returned to New Jersey, but once again, he was destined to leave. His career led him three years later to Nantucket, Massachusetts, where he became a chef at the Nantucket Country Club, and to Sturbridge Village. This

quaint New England village, which re-creates colonial America, is where he met Brenda.

Brenda worked as a banquet server in the Sturbridge Village and at the Sturbridge Hotel. She was born and raised in Puerto Rico and moved to Massachusetts when she was twenty-six years old. Brenda attended Johnson & Wales University in Providence, Rhode Island, with a focus on the art and discipline of baking. She began an apprenticeship with a renowned baker, with whom she further cultivated her craft. At one time, Brenda juggled three jobs: serving at two separate hotel restaurants while baking and decorating cakes on the side.

Henry and Brenda began dating during Henry's second season at Sturbridge Village. Shortly thereafter, Henry took a job in New Jersey and returned to his home state. The two tried long-distance dating, but Brenda made the trip to New Jersey a year later and stayed for good.

A NEW BEGINNING

It was after a twenty-hour shift on New Year's Eve that Henry decided he'd had enough with the restaurant business. He came home and said to Brenda, "I'm done. I can't do this every day. I quit." He was disheartened that he had spent the past decade working endless shifts for someone else. He wanted to be his own boss, to start his own business. He just didn't know exactly what that looked like—until he had the idea to open a food truck. Henry was ready to dive in, but Brenda paused; she would give him her full support only if he worked on someone else's truck and learned the industry first.

Soon after, Henry started working for Josh Sacks, owner of Oink and Moo BBQ, where he learned the ins and outs of food trucking. After two full seasons with Oink and Moo, Henry felt like he understood the business model and food trucks well enough to go out on his own. All the while, Henry and Brenda worked and saved. They threw every penny they had into starting a food truck. They developed their concept, customized their truck and were finally ready to hit the road in February 2017.

But the first year was a struggle. Henry and Brenda did everything, from greeting the guests to preparing the orders. They booked their events, ordered the inventory, prepped the meals, cleaned the truck inside and out—rinse and repeat every week. They couldn't be selective; they were new to the game and just learning the ropes. New food truckers don't get to be picky. During that first season, the couple took notes and ironed out the kinks. By their second season, Henry and Brenda knew the industry and how to prepare. Five years out, Cubano X-Press has become a northern New Jersey truck that patrons are elated to see at events and festivals throughout the tristate area.

Left to right: Tofu Picadillo (spicy) and Tofu Picadillo (regular).

PRESSING FORWARD

Cubano X-Press offers exactly what the name suggests. The truck specializes in a variety of Cuban sandwiches, as well as a few other Latin specialties with a twist. Their traditional Cubano includes marinated pork, ham and Swiss cheese, along with pickles, mustard and a drizzle of mojo sauce. Mojo is a popular Cuban sauce typically made from garlic and olive oil mixed with a citrus juice. Henry uses his own blend, however, which gives his sandwiches a distinct flavor. Likewise, their original Cubano Caliente sandwich adds pepperoni, spicy capicola and a Havana Heat Sauce. Though the dish is not spicy enough to mask the flavors of the pork, ham and mojo, it's still not for the faint of heart. Cubano X-Press also offers their Cuban sandwich with chicken instead of pork.

Henry strives to be creative in the kitchen while also staying true to traditional Latin cuisine. He likes to experiment and blend North American fare with his dishes. This creativity has birthed unique concoctions such as the Cubano Cheesesteak: thinly sliced steak with sofrito mayo, cheese sauce, caramelized onions and a lettuce and tomato salad. For sides, Cubano X-Press typically prepares fried plantains, ham croquettes and loaded yuca fries topped with a choice of pulled pork, chicken or roasted vegetables and chimichurri sauce. There's even a Cuban Nachos dish made from fried plantains, sofrito cheese sauce and the option of either pulled pork, chicken or roasted vegetables.

Cubano X-Press attends events from late winter to the holiday season every year. In between those festivals, Henry and Brenda cater a range of large private events, from birthday parties and corporate lunches to weddings and baby showers. Henry's vast experience and education enable him to customize any client's menu. Despite his constant prepping and cooking for the truck, Henry still loves to cook at home and come up with new recipes to try at events and catering gigs. Although he is a meat eater at heart, he often attempts a variety of vegan dishes, working solely with plants and tofu. It's the respect and care that Henry puts into these dishes that make them equally as enjoyable for meat eaters like him.

For example, Cubano X-Press's Tofu Picadillo is a popular pick for vegans and carnivores alike. Many Latin countries—as well as the Philippines—have their own spin on the dish. Traditionally, it's made with ground beef, tomatoes, potatoes and sometimes raisins and olives. Henry's version cuts out the meat and adds a slew of other fresh ingredients to his sauce. The recipe can be made with either regular or spicy tofu; however, the dish doesn't rely on either. Henry has conceived a vibrant, zesty sauce and paired the dish with a rice-and-bean combo.

Henry and Brenda are leaving the future of the business open-ended. They may add another truck to the fleet one day, or maybe they'll open a brick-and-mortar. They're not falling into any one track that would cement them in place. For now, they have their one truck and are soaking up every moment with it. One of the best parts of walking up to Cubano X-Press's window is seeing Brenda's smiling face while Henry blithely presses Cuban sandwiches on the grill. The two are constantly joking and laughing together. This was the type of career the couple spent years working toward. They're here now and don't have any regrets. After all, why concern yourself with the future when you're enjoying the moment?

Q&A WITH OWNERS HENRY SANCHEZ AND BRENDA ROSA

How was the transition from the world of restaurants to starting your own gourmet food truck?

Henry: It's way different from the restaurant. You have to be a lot more creative with your food. You have to be a lot more energetic. It's a different lifestyle than being out in a kitchen. During the time I worked for Josh, Brenda was working her butt off. We put every penny into the truck. And the first year was a struggle. The second year was good. The third year was great.

Brenda: In that first year, you're making so many mistakes. You get pickier—with events and those types of things—the second year. Eventually, you get to the point where you can pick events and spots that you want, what's good for you. You have to take so many things into consideration, and it's impossible to learn it all right away. It's really a learning process.

Henry: After the first two months on the truck, I came home and said to Brenda, "Are you going to quit your job? I need your helping running this truck." She quit her job, and we've been doing this since 2017. I do the manual work, and she does the administrative work, scheduling events, taking orders and prepping food.

Does Cubano X-Press offer catering?

Henry: We love catering parties and other events. They're always great experiences. We offer three distinct packages.

Brenda: We have the combo package; it's a flat rate per person, and you can choose a sandwich, a side and a drink or a platter. We have rice, beans, plantains for sides. Then we offer chicken, beef or vegetables. We also offer all you can eat, and that's a flat rate per person, too. And then you can rent out the truck for an hourly rate of $150. And we do all types of parties—weddings, birthdays; we did a communion recently.

What advice do you have for aspiring food truckers?

Henry: If you want to start a food truck…

Brenda: …go and work for another food truck.

Henry: That is the main advice. It's so important. That's how you can learn the business and learn if it's right for you. I have a good example for you: I have a friend who was interested in starting a food truck. I told him to come work with me to see what the industry is like. He worked two really busy days over a weekend last year, and I haven't heard from him since [laughs].

There are others who buy their food trucks before getting any experience out in the field, but they often don't last more than a season or two. People come to events and see you have a long line and look like you're making a lot of money. But they don't see you get up at five, six o'clock in the morning to start prepping Cubanos; they don't see you paying for permits or festival fees or your employees; they don't see you cleaning up after working an event for hours. It's a gamble to start a food truck, so it's really important to get some experience before opening your own.

Brenda: The other part of the advice is to have a concept.

Henry: Yes, that's important, too. Since the food truck is so different from a restaurant, it's important for you to develop your concept, what type of food you'll make and all that. It sets you apart from other trucks and really builds your identity.

CHAPTER 4

MS. FU'S YUMMY FOOD TRUCK

Lettuce Wrap

Mixed sweet peppers (1 each of red, yellow and orange peppers)
1 teaspoon rice vinegar
1 teaspoon salt
1 tablespoon cooking oil
1 cup chopped Napa cabbage
1 cup bean sprouts
2 tablespoons soy sauce
2 tablespoons cooking wine
1 garlic clove
1 teaspoon grated ginger
Choice of protein (¼ pound of either shredded rib-eye steak, shrimp, chicken or firm tofu)
A few leaves of romaine lettuce
1 scallion

Start by pickling peppers (for garnish). Slice each pepper into ⅛-inch, even slices and place into a bowl. Mix vinegar and salt into bowl with pepper slices. Cover bowl and place in fridge for at least 30 minutes.

In a wok or large skillet, add cooking oil over medium-high heat.

Chop Napa cabbage and add the chopped cabbage and bean sprouts to the skillet. Sautee for 2 to 3 minutes with 1 tablespoon of soy sauce and 1 tablespoon of cooking wine until veggies are almost tender.

In a separate pan on medium-high heat, pour in remaining soy sauce and cooking wine. Then throw in garlic clove and grated ginger. Cook protein of choice in this pan.

Combine the contents of the first skillet into the pan with protein. Stir well for 1 to 2 minutes.

Use lettuce leaves to make a cup and put mixture of protein and veggies into the lettuce cup.

Chop scallion.

Garnish lettuce wrap with pickled peppers and scallions.

Yakisoba Noodles

1 pack soft yakisoba noodles, steamed
1 tablespoon cooking oil
Choice of protein (¼ pound rib-eye steak, shrimp, chicken or firm tofu)
2 tablespoons soy sauce
2 tablespoons cooking wine
1 garlic clove

1 teaspoon grated ginger
1 cup chopped Napa cabbage
1 cup bean sprouts
1 tablespoon yakisoba sauce
1 scallion

Prepare noodles by steaming them until soft.

In a wok or large skillet over medium-high heat, add cooking oil. Cook protein of choice thoroughly with 1 tablespoon of soy sauce plus 1 tablespoon of cooking wine, garlic and ginger.

Add remaining soy sauce and cooking wine into the skillet with the protein.

Chop Napa cabbage and add the chopped cabbage and bean sprouts to the skillet. Sautee with protein 2 to 3 minutes until veggies are almost tender.

Add steamed noodles with yakisoba sauce to the skillet. Stir all the ingredients well.

Garnish with scallion and serve.

~~~

A Seven-Thousand-Mile Dream

Fumiji Aoki, or "Ms. Fu," as she is known by her son's friends, started life almost seven thousand miles away from New Jersey. She was born in Yokosuka, Japan, about an hour outside Tokyo, where her family now resides. Fumiji originally aspired to be a lawyer or businesswoman, but her teachers had other suggestions.

"They said, 'Well, you can be a great secretary,'" Fumiji recalls with a chuckle. "That's what I was told when I was in Japan."

Fumiji was always a tomboy growing up. She loved sports—and loudly voicing her opinions—but never felt like she fit in with Japanese culture. She loved her family and friends but couldn't see the future she wanted in Asia. So when she was seventeen years old, she came to the United States—specifically, Virginia—as a foreign exchange student. She quickly learned English, picking up various terms and phrases from her favorite TV shows and movies, from *Wayne's World* to *Beverly Hills, 90210*. Fumiji then attended Plymouth State University in New Hampshire. She cherished her American college experience, even earning a spot on a Plymouth promotional poster.

In 1998, Fumiji came to New Jersey and started with jobs in finance and banking. At home, however, she would regularly cook traditional Japanese cuisine for her family and friends. She soon became the designated honorary chef for events like birthday parties and social gatherings.

Starting Small...

After nearly two decades in finance, Fumiji was ready for a career change, one that suited her talent in the kitchen. In 2014, she began planning her food business, and by the following year, she was (literally) cooking. Unfortunately, her lack of experience in the field was immediately obvious, and she initially struggled to compete.

Fumiji didn't let adversity weigh her down. She took every challenge as a learning experience and overcame every problem she faced. She accepted criticism, considered suggestions and followed her gut. Soon enough, Ms.

Sukiyaki Cheese Steak Sandwich.

Fu's Yummy Food Truck had a custom wrap and was a staple at wine events and countless celebrations throughout the state.

Fumiji takes pride in her recipes and even adds her own twists to each of the dishes she creates. "I love Asian food, but I wanted to make it so that it's different but familiar at the same time," she says. "It's probably not authentic Japanese food. It has a lot of twists to it, like a cheesesteak."

In fact, Ms. Fu's Yummy Food Truck features basically everything Fumiji enjoys eating, from fried chicken wings and noodles to dumplings. She blends her favorite elements of Asian cuisines—including Chinese and Korean—into her dishes, using fresh ingredients to provide consistently high-quality meals.

...GROWING FAST

Fumiji believes her experiences on the food truck are invaluable. She also loves getting to work with her son, Taichi Rebele. As much as she appreciates the success of Ms. Fu's Yummy Food Truck, she cherishes the time she now spends with him, something that was missing during her time in the corporate world. While Fumiji is still a Certified Financial Planner, food trucking is her full-time profession. As partners, Fumiji and Taichi are now expanding their business partnership.

In 2022, the mother-and-son team founded Bebop Food Truck, an Asian fusion taco truck. Taichi heads the operations of Bebop, as Fumiji continues to head Ms. Fu's. Though the two once again expect some trials and tribulations, their teamwork and familiarity with the industry will help smooth out the process.

When Fumiji moved to the United States, she wasn't exactly searching for the American dream. She was looking to create her own dream, to live life on her own terms and to follow her individual path without interference. Through diligence and determination, she has followed the "Fumiji dream," one filled with happiness and success. Whether she has to travel seven thousand miles or grind for seven thousand days, Fumiji has proven she can forge her own way.

Q&A with Owner Fumiji Aoki

Where are you from in Japan?

Tokyo. I was born and raised in Yokosuka, but my family is in Tokyo now.

What were your experiences like in Japan prior to coming to America?

I always make a joke that I was deported because I did not fit into Japanese culture. I was told, "Know your place." That was the line that I heard all my life. So I left my place. It wasn't there.

It was too much. I got into trouble. And my teacher used to say to my mother, "She does not act like a girl." So it was a problem, because I always wanted to be one of the boys. I didn't want to be one of the boys, really—I just wanted to say whatever I wanted to say, just like boys. I wanted to play all the sports.

There were so many of us, like, a lot of Japanese exchange students in the '90s. A lot of us who felt like we needed more opportunities. A lot of us left to different countries at the time.

Do you ever go back and visit?

Every year since I had my son twenty years ago.

What made you start your own food truck?

I love food, and I love to eat, mainly [laughs]. I love to eat. And I feel like happiness comes from eating food, hanging out with good people. So I always cook for all the family members and all the family birthday parties and get-togethers.

And I was burned out from finance. I just couldn't get up in the morning and do that again. And food is simple—good food and everybody's happy.

What was your first season like?

I wasn't in the food industry before starting a food truck. So I didn't know how to put the fryer on. I didn't know how to do the pilot for the grill. I YouTube'd everything and learned everything [laughs]. I didn't know what worked, what did not work.

The first season was rough, and I learned a lot of lessons. I had a lot of fun and a lot of pain. I'm going through that again right now. I have a second truck, and it's going to be different cuisine. So I'm going through another pain, too, just like the first year. I'm asking for punishment; I don't know why [laughs].

What's your cuisine like on Ms. Fu's Yummy Food Truck?

I love Asian food, but I wanted to make it so that it's different but familiar at the same time. We have Asian flavor cheesesteak. It has rib-eye on Portuguese bread. And also I like Chinese food. I like Korean food. So fusion usually means, like, cross-culture, but mostly Asian. So I think it's fun.

What are some fan-favorite items?

Yakisoba noodles is definitely our staple, but we use special salt that is different than other Japanese places. So I think it has Japanese flavor but with a twist, too. And we have pork buns. We are doing Korean kimchi tacos, and we have the chicken nuggets and Japanese tacos.

What are some of your favorite events to attend throughout the year?

We do a lot of wine events. I think wine people understand our food a little more because we're a little bit more sophisticated. We spend a lot of money on buying the rib-eye steak, and we understand how to make vegan and vegetarian options available to them. We try to keep it fresh, keep it quality.

Did being born and raised in Japan influence your truck's cuisine?

Yeah! Because in Japan…I always think that Japanese people make a lot of different cuisine better. Like Japanese ramen. Ramen comes from China, definitely. But I think when I eat the noodles, Japanese ramen is the best [laughs].

It was so funny because I wanted Korean barbecue. But Japanese Korean barbecue, we don't want to say refined, but we have our own improvement. And when you eat in Japan, I think Tokyo has more Michelin stars than any other place in the world. So when you go anywhere, you can find the best of everything, even convenience, like Japanese 7 Eleven. They will have single cups of coffee. They grind it right there and brew the coffee right there. In Japan, you're told to care about everything you do. Every single thing you do, you should care about what you put into it. So it's good and bad [laughs]. I think I want to be the best of both worlds. I don't want to be that uptight. I want my son to also have fun but also be proud of what he's doing.

What kind of catering options do you offer with Ms. Fu's Yummy Food Truck?

We do a lot of private events—weddings, corporate lunches, corporate dinners. We do a lot of bar mitzvahs. We can do a lot of vegan options, too. There's not a lot of vegan-only trucks, so we can be the vegan truck for an event or offer vegan options. It's easy for us to do that.

CHAPTER 5

THE BROWNIE BAR

Massimo's (non)Gingerbread Cookies

Makes 9 cookies

1 cup all-purpose flour
2 tablespoons Dutch cocoa powder
1 teaspoon cream of tartar
½ teaspoon baking soda
¼ teaspoon salt
1 stick unsalted butter, softened
¾ cup granulated sugar, plus 2 tablespoons for rolling
1 large egg
½ tablespoon ground cinnamon

Preheat oven to 400 degrees Fahrenheit. Line one sheet pan with parchment paper.

Whisk together flour, cocoa powder, cream of tartar, baking soda and salt in a small bowl, then set aside.

With a hand mixer, cream butter and sugar together in a large bowl until light and fluffy. Scrape sides of bowl with a runner spatula. Beat in the egg until combined. Add dry ingredients and beat at low speed until just combined.

In a small bowl, mix remaining 2 tablespoons of sugar with cinnamon.

Measure out about 2 tablespoons of dough and roll into 9 balls. Roll balls in cinnamon sugar and place on prepared sheet pan, spacing them about 2 inches apart.

Bake 9 to 11 minutes in the center of the oven until edges are beginning to set and centers are soft and puffy. If doubling the recipe, prepare cookie dough on the second sheet pan while the first pan is baking. The cookies bake better one sheet at a time.

Let cookies cool on baking sheet for 2 minutes before transferring them to a cooling rack. Serve warm or at room temperature.

SWEET ON YOU

Any time is a good time to have a brownie. The soft and dense chocolate treat is delectable on its own but even better when paired with other goodies. Which is exactly what the husband-and-wife team behind the Brownie Bar specializes in.

Lai and Gustavo Barboni met twenty years ago in New York City. Although they worked in the Big Apple, they both commuted to the city from their homes in northern New Jersey. In particular, Lai was born in Weehawken and raised in western New York. Her family eventually moved to Ridgefield, but Lai found her own apartment the next town over and hasn't left Bergen County since. Meanwhile, Gustavo was born in Argentina and moved to Jersey City to live with his aunt in 1995.

The couple first met working together at the original (now closed) Blue Smoke barbecue restaurant in the Flatiron District. Lai was a pastry cook and Gustavo the head bartender. The two connected through food and their appreciation of finding and creating new, unique recipes.

In fact, as one of their first interactions, Lai was preparing to dispose of some excess liquid from macerated strawberries and rhubarb when Gustavo stopped her. He took the enormous container of pink liquid and returned with a cocktail: Strawberry-Rhubarb Caipiroska, a twist on a Caipirinha but made with vodka instead of cachaça. What was otherwise about to be disposed of instead became a deliciously sweet and refreshing drink. The two soon began dating before marrying in 2005.

Ready to take on a new endeavor after marriage, Gustavo came home one day with a food trailer complete with an oven. At the time, the couple was working full-time jobs; Gustavo was simply looking for a side gig he could work with his wife. Their initial plan was to sell empanadas. But by then, the industry was saturated with empanada trucks, and the Barbonis struggled to find festivals and locations at which to vend.

Triple Chocolate Brownie.

Caramel Sea Salt Brownie.

Lai had the idea to try sweets. She suggested to her husband they change their concept to a dessert truck. At first, the couple settled on cupcakes, but before they pulled the trigger, they decided against it. Established cupcake trucks were popular, and the couple feared they'd face the same fate as their empanada plan. So Lai asked herself, "What sweet treat is simple to make—like a cookie—and can have different flavor variations but be familiar and nostalgic like a cupcake?" The answer: brownies!

BAKE, TASTE, REPEAT

Lai spent months developing her brownie recipe. She had an idea of how she wanted to make them, but she wanted to ensure that they would be deeply rich and simple to make. Once she pinned down her brownie recipe, she began brainstorming flavor variations. She and Gustavo wanted to make traditional flavors as well as options no other bakery carries. Using Gustavo's bartending knowledge and Lai's pastry skills, the couple developed some Boozy Brownies, including their White Russian brownie and Mojito blondie. From there, they created their signature s'mores, pecan pie and caramel sea salt flavors and still continue to experiment with new flavors.

Lai and Gustavo spent about five years with the truck before they decided to open a café. After dedicating more and more time to the Brownie Bar, Lai was ready to leave her other job behind. In addition, several pleasantly hectic and successful seasons gave them the idea to open a dedicated storefront. This also allowed them to expand their menu, offering more than just brownies.

At the Brownie Bar Café in Ridgefield Park, Bergen County, guests can pair their brownies with caffeinated beverages such as espresso, cappuccino, latte, tea and freshly brewed coffee, as well as a number of seasonal options. Besides brownies, Lai whips up specialty sundaes. Of course, there's no shortage of brownie flavors, with a rotating list that includes favorites like triple chocolate, cookies and cream and Funfetti.

Every item sold by the Brownie Bar is handcrafted using the best available ingredients. Lai prides herself on baking with 100 percent cacao chocolate, Dutch cocoa powder, European-style butter, cane sugar and fresh herbs, fruits and vegetables. The brownies come out soft and gooey, the chocolate full-bodied and sumptuous. Lai and Gustavo bring an originality to their products and are always developing diverse alternatives to traditional confections. Looking at the menu, it's difficult not to ask for one of everything.

Q&A WITH CO-FOUNDER LAI BARBONI

What different items can people get from your truck?
Besides seasonal brownies and blondies, in the warmer months people can find homemade vanilla ice cream for a brownie à la mode or a brownie sundae topped with homemade sauces and fresh whipped cream. We also have beverages like cold brew coffee, spiced apple cider and our extravagant Frozen Chocolate Blast, which is an over-the-top chocolate slushee! We're also working on a nondairy, tropical fruit version of the Blast.

What can patrons expect from a Brownie Bar brownie?
They can definitely expect a rich, fudgy brownie. The blondies are a bit cakier but still moist and chewy and not crumbly.

What was business like when you started out?
It was difficult. We thought we could just park on a street somewhere and start selling, kind of like in New York City. Soon we realized every town has

different rules pertaining to food trucks, and some towns don't even allow them. We had to rely on companies that produce festivals and street fairs, but then it would get expensive, with not only the application fees but health and fire permit fees for every town. Eventually, people started seeking us out for private catering. People would constantly ask if we had a permanent location where they could get their brownie fix. This is one of the reasons why we decided to open a brick-and-mortar.

What kind of catering options do you offer?

We serve mini brownie trios with optional beverages and/or ice cream. Guests get to choose from a menu of flavors, which people love to do. It gives them a chance to taste different things. Our dessert food truck is available for private catering, weddings, corporate functions, school events, religious celebrations and fundraisers. If you don't need the truck and just want brownies, you can order trays at the Brownie Bar Café.

What can you tell us about the café?

The café is part bakery, part coffee shop, part sit-down eatery. We basically needed a full commercial kitchen of our own to support and expand the food truck. But we wanted our neighbors and customers to have a place to hang out and enjoy a good cup of coffee with a fresh baked sweet.

PART II

....

CENTRAL JERSEY FOOD TRUCKS

....

6. Bearded One BBQ
Recipe: Brisket Grilled Cheese
Biography
Q&A with Owner Chris D'Addario

7. Big John's Gourmet Burgers
Recipe: Mac and Cheese Burger
Recipe: Sunny Side Up Burger
Biography
Q&A with Owner Jonathan Anderson

8. House of Cupcakes
Recipe: Espresso Dark Brownie Cupcakes with Peanut Butter
Fudge Frosting
Recipe: Oatmeal Raisin Cupcakes with Orange Cream Cheese Icing
Biography
Q&A with Owner Ron Bzdewka and Son Rage Bzdewka

9. Maddalena's CheeseCake & Catering
Recipe: Frozen Chookie Cookie
Biography
Q&A with Co-Founder Janet Maddalena

10. The Mexi-Boys
Recipe: Pico de Gallo
Recipe: Salsa Verde
Biography
Q&A with Co-Owner Eduardo Rojas

CHAPTER 6

BEARDED ONE BBQ

Brisket Grilled Cheese

Brisket
Brisket (desired size and trim)
Dry rub (as desired)

Grilled Cheese
2 slices Texas toast (per sandwich)
Salted butter (as desired)
¼ cup shredded Monterey cheddar (per slice of Texas toast)
Sweet barbecue sauce (as desired)

Brisket: Preheat oven to 250 degrees Fahrenheit. Trim off all membrane and reduce down the fat on the back side of the brisket. Coat meat in dry rub of choice, making sure to cover entire brisket. Add meat to smoker or oven and cook for approximately 8 to 9 hours, until meat is tender. Remove brisket from smoker or oven and let rest for 30 to 60 minutes. This allows the juices to settle back into the meat.

Grilled Cheese: While the brisket rests, prepare your grilled cheese. Heat a pan on the stove at medium-high to approximately 350 degrees Fahrenheit. Coat only one side of bread with butter. Repeat for each slice of bread. Lay bread slices in pan—butter side down—and cover each slice of bread with approximately ¼ cup of cheese. Cover pan for

several seconds to help cheese melt; thicker slices of bread slow down the melting process. Put barbecue sauce on each slice of bread.

Assemble: Cut three to four slices of brisket, cutting against the grain. Add sliced brisket to one slice of bread (already coated with cheese and barbecue sauce). Use second slice of bread (already coated with cheese and barbecue sauce) to cover the slice with brisket once bottom is a golden-brown color. Remove from stove and enjoy!

~~~

THIS PIG CAN FLY

In a pocket off Route 33 in Monroe Township, a lone monochrome trailer is parked in a gravel lot. Stacked behind it, barely in sight, is a wall of logs destined for death row. If you're buzzing down the highway, you might miss the one-thousand-gallon smoker on the shoulder or the giant pink-and-silver banner emblazoned with images of bearded pigs. But what's impossible to miss are the curtains of smoke billowing from even larger smokers behind the trailer.

This is no Burning Man event; it's just Pitmaster Chris D'Addario—the man behind Bearded One BBQ—preparing his award-winning pork, beef and chicken.

The scents are what hit you first. Cherry logs chewed by the flame kiss, then char, the homemade rubs that coat the meat; racks of St. Louis ribs, mounds of pork shoulder, heaps of chicken wings and prime cuts of beef brisket line the chambers of every smoker. Still, it's not enough food for the hordes who haunt Bearded One BBQ every Tuesday through Saturday.

Chris's parking lot fills up fast, as cars swiftly file along the shoulder of Route 33 in front of his trailer to reach what's appropriately referred to as "The Spot." Guests come to grab catering trays to-go and swallow an entire brisket grilled cheese sandwich before they make it back to their cars. Outdoor dining is offered at several picnic tables scattered in a woodchip bed behind the smokers. Edison bulbs and tiny rubber pigs are strung around the perimeter.

Chris and his wife, Jess, began their food trucking enterprise nearly a decade ago. It was a hobby that grew into competing in—then winning—regional events. While still employed full time, Chris and Jess decided to take Bearded One on the road in 2016 to vend at festivals around the state. For the next few years, Bearded One BBQ was a staple at events throughout northern and central New Jersey. If you ever had trouble locating them, all you had to do was look for the longest line, as chances were they were at the other end of it.

OFF-ROADING

In 2019, Chris found an available lot off the highway in Monroe. It had enough room for his trailer, some smokers, a picnic area and even a second truck for the occasional guest to vend dessert. Before the spring of 2020, The Spot was in action. Chris and his team began smoking full time on the side of the road, and they haven't slowed down since.

As a result of The Spot's success, Bearded One has since slowed their attendance at events, only vending at a handful in a given year. Much of their attention is also devoted to on-site catering. This catering option— perfect for parties—allows patrons to choose from a long list of items.

Though the truck's menu grows every season, Chris stays true to the heart of barbecue. He'll get creative, but every bite sizzles with that smoky tang of signature Bearded One flavor. In the beginning, the blackboard menu would have a few listed specials such as brisket, pulled pork and ribs. Those in the know would add their brisket or pulled pork to a grilled cheese or pile them atop a cup of mac and cheese. Since then, Bearded One has added tacos, quesadillas and burgers. Chris's signature dry-rub, smoke-fried wings are also a hit for football Sundays.

Bearded One BBQ offers both on-site catering for larger events and takeaway trays for smaller parties. Guests have several packages of meats, sides and rolls to choose from for on-site catering for parties of fifty or more.

Left to right: Brisket Grilled Cheese and Pulled Pork Grilled Cheese.

For smaller social gatherings, Chris personally prepares any combination of trays with your choice of pulled pork or chicken, beef brisket, wings, chili, mac and cheese, sausage and peppers, plus a selection of sides.

Makin' Bacon

Chris now devotes all of his professional time to the food truck. It's an enterprise he started with his wife and continues to build with his son, Connor; however, the latter is still young and prefers to eat brisket grilled cheese sandwiches rather than make them. Prior to Bearded One, Chris was working an office job with little thought that his side gig barbecuing could be a legitimate venture. Now he's got a constant line of cars telling him otherwise, and he's on a career path that enables him to spend countless hours with his family.

Nearly every day you can catch the pitmaster ricocheting from smoker to smoker, tossing logs into the fireboxes and checking on the fare. You'll recognize him by his voluminous jet-black (he says "grayish") beard. He's typically busy barbecuing for the line of ravenous carnivores that doesn't die down until close—or until he's out of food. Of course, Jess and Connor often visit to lend a hand or moral support. What began as a hobby is now a full-time family business.

Q&A with Owner Chris D'Addario

How did Bearded One BBQ come about?

It was a hobby that grew out of hand. It started out with a little grill and a little bigger smoker; then a really big smoker; then multiple smokers; then eventually a twenty-foot trailer with basically everything. We started doing competitions. Then we realized this costs a lot of money, so we started vending. So it grew organically from horrible competitions to winning grand champions.

Do you have any barbecue education or professional culinary experience?

Zero. I just love to cook and mess around. Then your friends will tell you your cooking's really good, and you don't believe them; but when you keep

hearing it, you think, "Well, maybe I have something here." And that's when we started entering competitions.

What was the business like when you started out?

A mess. The first real festival we did was the Beer, BBQ & Bacon Showdown in 2016. That was our first one, and that was extremely busy, but we had no idea what we were doing. After that, we got more equipment, more products. Jess D'Addario: Yeah, that was a big eye-opener. But he did make a name for himself when he won "Best BBQ" that year.

What do you attribute your success to?

I think it's a little bit of everything. We always try to cook the same way, whether it's for a competition or for an event. And I think that is beneficial. In 2017, I had to have cooked more than thirty thousand pounds of brisket, and that helps me work more efficiently and always make my food consistent. Now it's just second nature—as well as practice. And winning competitions doesn't hurt either [laughs].

What would you say is the most popular item on your menu?

What would *you* say is the most popular?

Brisket grilled cheese!

You got it [laughs]!

CHAPTER 7
BIG JOHN'S GOURMET BURGERS

Mac and Cheese Burger

5 pounds ground chuck (makes 12 7-ounce burgers)
2½ teaspoons cumin
1½ teaspoons coriander
1 teaspoon salt (kosher preferred)
½ teaspoon pepper (a dash)
2½ teaspoons mint leaves
1 cup olive oil
Mac and cheese (based on preference)
Brioche bun

In a large bowl, mix the ground beef and add cumin, coriander, salt, pepper, mint leaves and olive oil. Mix thoroughly.

Once mixed, measure out 7 ounces of ground beef and form into a burger patty. Cook burger in a large pan or skillet on medium heat for 3 minutes on each side or longer (based on preference.)

Cook preferred mac and cheese based on recommended instructions.

Place burger on brioche bun and apply a decent amount of mac and cheese on top.

Enjoy.

～

Sunny Side Up Burger

5 pounds ground chuck (makes 12 7-ounce burgers)
2½ teaspoons cumin
1½ teaspoons coriander
1 teaspoon salt (kosher preferred)
½ teaspoon pepper (a dash)
2½ teaspoons mint leaves
1 cup olive oil
1 egg
1 slice cheddar cheese
1 brioche bun
Lettuce
Tomato slices
Chopped onions
Pickles (pickle chips preferred)

In a large bowl, mix the ground beef and add cumin, coriander, salt, pepper, mint leaves and olive oil. Mix thoroughly.

Once mixed, measure out 7 ounces of ground beef and form into a burger patty. Cook burger in a large pan or skillet on medium heat for 3 minutes on each side or longer (based on preference.)

Using a separate pan or skillet over low heat, crack egg into pan or skillet and cook until the white is completely set but the yolk remains runny, approximately 2 to 2½ minutes.

When the burger is almost completely cooked, apply cheddar cheese until cheese is melted.

Place the burger on brioche bun and add sunny side egg, lettuce, tomato, onions and pickles.

Enjoy.

～

Mexican Street Corn from Carlitos Barbecue Taqueria (see pages 18–24).

Left to right: Pulled Pork Quesataco, Brisket Quesataco and Sweet Plantain Quesataco from Carlitos Barbecue Taqueria (see pages 18–24).

Left to right: Spicy Orange Wings, Waffle Fries with Cheese Sauce and Chicken Sliders from Chick Wings & Things (see pages 25–30).

Left to right: the Cubano, Cubano BLT and Cubano Cheesesteak from Cubano X-Press (see pages 31–39).

Owner Fumiji Aoki in front of Ms. Fu's Yummy Food Truck (see pages 40–47).

Brownies from the Brownie Bar (see pages 48–53).

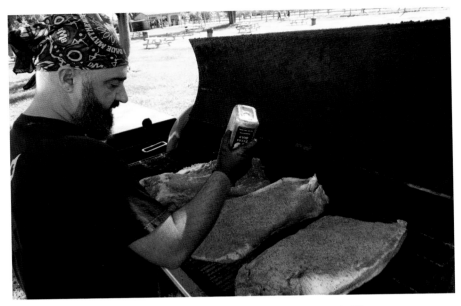

Chris D'Addario of Bearded One BBQ using a smoker (see pages 56–61).

Hot dog from Big John's Gourmet Burgers (see pages 62–69).

Big John's Gourmet Burgers food truck (see pages 62–69).

Ice Cream Sundae Cupcakes from House of Cupcakes (see pages 70–78).

Janet Maddalena from Maddalena's CheeseCake & Catering (see pages 79–86).

Chookie Cookie from Maddalena's CheeseCake & Catering (see pages 79–86).

Eduardo Rojas from the Mexi-Boys (see pages 87–92).

Nachos from the Mexi-Boys (see pages 87–92).

The Miller family from Five Sisters Food Co. (see pages 94–100).

Left to right: Surf N Turf, Jersey and Whiskey Tango sandwiches from Five Sisters Food Co. (see pages 94–100).

John Fels from Jersey Roll cooking on his truck (see pages 101–106).

Pork roll sandwich with tater tots from Jersey Roll (see pages 101–106).

Day boat scallops and shrimp combo with wasabi mashed potatoes and mango chutney from Ohana Food Truck (see pages 107–116).

Co-owner/head chef James Costello from Ohana Food Truck (see pages 107–116).

The team from Shore Good Eats 'N' Treats (see pages 117–125).

Ice cream cookie sandwiches from Kiersten's Creations (see pages 126–133).

Traditional peanut butter chocolate mousse and cold brew float from Kiersten's Creations (see pages 126–133).

Daniel Hover from Dan's Waffles making a BBQ Pulled Pork Waffle (see pages 136–145).

Daniel Hover from Dan's Waffles (see pages 136–145).

Emily Hodecker from Good Food = Good Mood (see pages 146–152).

Mac Burger from Good Food = Good Mood (see pages 146–152).

Desiree Bagnell from the Grateful Gourmet (see pages 153–159).

Clockwise from bottom left: Friend of the Deviled Eggs, Celestial Mac and Cheese, Hell in a Bucket Hot Chicken Sandwich, Googie Dog and Franklin's Brussels from the Grateful Gourmet (see pages 153–159).

Mama Dude's food truck (see pages 160–168).

Top: Build-your-own bowls from Mama Dude's (see pages 160–168).

Middle: Owner Cindy Matas from Surf and Turf (see pages 169–174).

Bottom: *Left to right*: Warm Lobster Roll, BLT Lobster Roll and Crab Roll from Surf and Turf (see pages 169–174).

A *BIG* DECISION

Jonathan Anderson has spent his life bouncing around the Garden State. Born in Jersey City, he relocated to Plainfield with his family when he was in elementary school. But before high school, he and his family moved again to Piscataway. After graduation, Jonathan joined the United States Navy, leaving his home state to serve his country for several years. He says his time in the navy taught him the discipline and skills he continues to utilize in his career.

After the navy, Jonathan moved to Edison. He enrolled at DeVry Technical School and earned a degree in computer information systems. Upon graduating, Jonathan started a career in information technology in 1995, soon earning a job at *Time* magazine. He worked for Time Inc., the former mass media corporation, where his duties mainly consisted of support and development. In 2002, Jonathan returned to Plainfield, where he remains to this day.

Every day on Sixth Avenue in New York City, Jonathan watched as food trucks parked themselves outside his office building. He noticed that as soon as the windows swung open, lines would form, and the trucks would stay frenzied even well past lunchtime. In the back of his mind, he considered starting his own food truck but never acted on it. After all, he had a fruitful career working for an internationally revered brand. He wasn't interested in testing the waters just yet.

Jonathan spent nearly seventeen years with *Time* magazine before his unit was dissolved. Time Inc. changed hands several times before ultimately being acquired by the competing Meredith Corporation media company, with Time Inc.'s IT unit among the casualties.

GO YOUR OWN WAY

Jonathan always admired the idea of food truckers being their own bosses—no one to answer to but themselves. You sank or swam on your own. Being a military man, Jonathan was determined to put his skills and perseverance to use in a brand-new endeavor where he could call the shots. He dove into the food trucking world headfirst under the moniker of his lifelong nickname, "Big John."

The concept came first. As a burger lover, Jonathan has spent a lifetime trying different recipes, with various spices, seasonings and beef blends. He

decided to use this knowledge to develop a concise menu for his food truck, and soon Big John's Gourmet Burgers was born. The goal was to serve a burger that was tasty without a bun or any toppings. After dozens and dozens of variations, his family members and friends came to a consensus of their favorite recipe. The result of their decision is still the same recipe the truck uses today.

Jonathan's special seven-ounce Angus chuck burgers served on brioche buns were a hit from day one. The only problem was an overall lack of foot traffic. Big John's Gourmet Burgers first opened at the start of the new year, meaning it debuted *before* the typical start of the food trucking season. As a result, his first couple months were terribly slow. Luckily, by that first spring, Jonathan was finding his audience. He started attending events in central and northern New Jersey, mostly at parks, youth sports and local school fairs. He started receiving catering requests to supply food for corporate lunches and became a popular food truck around Union County.

BEEFING UP

Since his debut, Jonathan has expanded his menu to feature more than seven different burger options. Big John's now offers a barbecue bacon burger topped with onion rings, a chili cheese burger, a mushroom Swiss and a bleu cheese burger, as well as a vegan burger. Other fan favorites include the Mac and Cheese Burger and the Sunny Side Burger; the latter is topped with cheese, bacon and one egg sunny side up. Of course, he also offers basic hamburger or cheeseburger options. Jonathan's signature burger, however, is the California burger, with cheese, lettuce, tomato, onion and pickle.

Jonathan has enjoyed being his own boss. He creates all his menu items, manages the truck and handles all of the administrative work, social media and bookings. He also has the ability to call on his dedicated friends, who are happy to lend a hand whenever Jonathan needs them. As the face of Big John's Gourmet Burgers, Jonathan has to endure the struggles and celebrate the successes alike all on his own. But he answers only to himself, and that's just the way he likes it.

Q&A WITH OWNER JONATHAN ANDERSON

Where is your truck based?

I would have to say my main base is Union. I'm here every Thursday. And last season was probably my most constant, every Thursday. Otherwise, I do a lot of catered events. I was pretty popular this year up and down Route 22. I did a lot of corporate office events, private catering events, school events, school sporting events. So when people ask me, "Where are you?" I say, "Come to Union on Thursdays."

What gave you the idea to do a truck?

I worked right there at Sixth Avenue, Avenue of the Americas, right across from Radio City, and I would see all the food trucks pull up there for lunch for three hours. And I thought, "Wow, these guys are really doing well. They're their own boss, you know, and they're all doing well and they're pulling out of here." And I'm just trying to guesstimate how well they would do, because they would keep a long line for three hours. So I started researching while I was still working at *Time*, just looking at the cost of food trucks and how much it would cost to get something like that going, how you would operate it. I didn't know anything about it.

And I thought, "Yeah, I'd like to start a food truck." I've always had a thing for burgers. I would drive forty-five minutes to find a good burger. I have Angus chuck as my burger. Chuck steak makes a great-tasting burger,

so I found the burger and I press my own burgers. I don't buy frozen burger patties. They're actually big giant burgers. I have a seven-ounce burger, so it's a nice-sized burger on a brioche bun. Fresh toppings and a distinct taste.

Is the bacon cheeseburger your most popular?

Yeah, when people come up to the truck, a lot of people go with what they know. So cheeseburger, bacon cheeseburger, depending on where I am. Some burgers are more popular than others. Like, I can go to one part of New Jersey, and everybody wants a mushroom Swiss. And I can go to another part, and everybody wants the sunny side. Usually when I go into towns where people are a little more affluent, you know, they're going for the popular expensive burgers. They want the mac and cheese, they want the sunny side. So there are a lot more people that are willing to take a chance and sample something they haven't had.

Do you offer any seasonal burgers or event-specific menu items?

I have a nice variety, and I usually stick with that. I do offer a hot dog as well. I have a fried chicken sandwich, and I have cheese fries with either chili on it or bacon.

Tell us about your catering.

I have three packages. One is a basic. Then I have a plus, and then I have a deluxe. Deluxe is my entire menu, which includes cheese fries, every burger that I have, the chicken sandwich, everything. My basic is not every burger but my more popular burgers. It's the bacon cheeseburger, bleu cheeseburger and the fries and my onion rings. Then I have a plus menu, which is in the middle, where you get the cheese fries, you know, added to that and you get a couple more burgers, like a chili cheese and a mushroom Swiss.

What are some of your favorite events to attend throughout the year?

I had a lot of success in Union this year. I do a lot of sporting events for kids, like lacrosse and soccer, and a lot of outdoor events. Kids love burgers, so when they see the burger on the side of my truck, they come running [laughs]. And I like doing school events as well as street festivals and food truck events. I like doing food truck–specific events where it's like a wine and beer garden added as a hook to get people in and you have a series of really good food trucks. I usually do well at those.

What advice would you give a young food trucker?

I would say whatever your specialty is, perfect that. Don't try to do too many different things. And stay consistent. It's hard to be consistent, you know, so be consistent with what you serve, how you do it. This is why McDonald's and Burger King work. People know what they're going to get before they walk in the door because they stay consistent—with the flavor, the taste, the menu. So be consistent!

CHAPTER 8

HOUSE OF CUPCAKES

Espresso Dark Brownie Cupcakes
with Peanut Butter Fudge Frosting

Dark Brownie Cupcakes
1 cup unsalted butter, cut into pieces
4 ounces unsweetened chocolate, chopped
1 cup all-purpose flour
¼ cup unsweetened Dutch-process cocoa powder, sifted
2 tablespoons finely ground espresso
¼ teaspoon salt
1¾ cups packed brown sugar
½ cup granulated sugar
4 large eggs

Peanut Butter Fudge Frosting
¾ cup unsalted butter, room temperature
½ cup creamy peanut butter
Pinch of salt
2 cups confectioners' sugar
¾ cup unsweetened Dutch-process cocoa powder

For Dark Brownie Cupcakes: Preheat the oven to 350 degrees Fahrenheit. Line standard cupcake pans with 24 cupcake liners.

Combine the butter and chocolate in a small microwave-safe bowl. Microwave on high, uncovered, stirring every 30 seconds, until the butter and chocolate are melted and smooth. Set aside to cool.

Mix the flour, cocoa powder, espresso and salt in another bowl.

Using the bowl of an electric mixer fitted with the paddle attachment, mix both sugars and reserved chocolate mixture until well combined. Add eggs, 1 at a time, beating until each is smooth, scraping down the sides of the bowl if needed. Add the flour mixture until blended.

Fill the cupcake liners two-thirds full.

Bake until golden, rotating the pans halfway through, for 18 to 20 minutes.

Transfer the pans to wire racks to cool completely before removing the cupcakes.

For Peanut Butter Fudge Frosting: Using the bowl of an electric mixer fitted with the paddle attachment, beat the butter, peanut butter and salt on medium-high speed until creamy.

Turn the speed to low and beat in the confectioners' sugar, ½ cup at a time. Add the cocoa powder and beat until extremely smooth and creamy.

Assembly: Frost the cooled cupcakes with Peanut Butter Fudge Frosting and enjoy.

~~~

Oatmeal Raisin Cupcakes with Orange Cream Cheese Icing

Oatmeal Raisin Cupcakes
3¾ cups old-fashioned rolled oats, divided
2½ cups all-purpose flour
⅔ cup oat bran
½ teaspoon baking soda
1½ teaspoons baking powder
1 teaspoon salt
2 teaspoons ground cinnamon
1½ cups unsalted butter, room temperature
1 cup granulated sugar
1 cup packed light brown sugar
4 large eggs
2 teaspoons pure vanilla extract
1 cup sour cream
1½ cups raisins
1 cup sweetened flaked coconut

Orange Cream Cheese Icing
4 ounces cream cheese, room temperature
½ cup unsalted butter, room temperature
Pinch of salt
2½ cups confectioners' sugar, sifted
2 teaspoons grated orange zest
2 teaspoons orange-flavored liqueur or extract

For the Oatmeal Raisin Cupcakes: Preheat the oven to 375 degrees Fahrenheit. Line standard cupcake pans with 36 cupcake liners.

Whisk 2 cups of oats with the flour, oat bran, baking soda, baking powder, salt and cinnamon in a medium bowl.

Using the bowl of an electric mixer fitted with the paddle attachment, cream the butter and both sugars on medium-high speed until pale and fluffy. Add the eggs, 1 at a time, beating until each is smooth, scraping

down the sides of the bowl if needed. Beat in the vanilla. Turn the speed to low, add the flour mixture and beat until combined. Beat in the sour cream. Stir in the raisins by hand.

Transfer 2¾ cups of batter to a small bowl, and then stir in the coconut and the remaining 1¾ cups of oats. Divide the plain batter among the cupcake liners, and then top each with 1 tablespoon of oat-coconut batter.

Bake until golden, rotating the pans halfway through, for 18 to 20 minutes. Then transfer the pans to wire racks to cool completely before removing the cupcakes.

For the Orange Cream Cheese Icing: Using the bowl of an electric mixer fitted with the paddle attachment, beat the cream cheese, butter and salt on medium-high speed until creamy. Turn the speed to low and beat in the confectioners' sugar, ½ cup at a time. Increase the speed to medium-high and beat until light and fluffy.

Add the orange zest and liqueur, beating steadily until mixed.

Refrigerate the frosting for 30 to 60 minutes to firm.

Assembly: Frost the cooled cupcakes with Orange Cream Cheese Icing and enjoy.

～

Mad about Cupcakes

Ron and Ruthie Bzdewka, along with their young sons Rage and Riot, started their family business in 2008. Ruthie—a lifelong baker—found a little vacant shop on Witherspoon Street in Princeton, just a short walk from Nassau Street. After years of developing and perfecting her own recipes, she was ready to open a bakery.

Ron and Ruthie developed the business concept together. They decided that Ruthie's cupcakes would be the focal point, but they also wanted to offer pastries and other treats like cookies and chocolate-covered pretzels. The plan was to offer an expansive selection of cupcakes, including flavors people couldn't make at home or find at any other bakery. After finalizing the menu, renovating the shop and building the staff, House of Cupcakes officially opened in 2008.

And then the Great Recession hit. It took some time, but House of Cupcakes was able to survive, and eventually thrive, building a massive following in the process. Patrons love that the shop's cupcakes are always fresh and made from scratch.

Drafted for War

A year after House of Cupcakes opened, Ron received an email from the producers of Food Network's *Cupcake Wars*. He deleted it. They sent him another message. He deleted that one, too. Then Ron got a phone call from an unknown number. He answered it, and the man on the other line invited him to audition for *Cupcake Wars*. It was being developed for cable as a reality competition series in which contestants would face off in separate challenges, and one contestant would be eliminated each round. The winner would receive $10,000.

The family auditioned for the competition and were selected to participate. Ron and Ruthie flew out to Los Angeles, California, to film their segment, taking on three other bakers and coming out victorious after three rounds. Ron and Ruthie returned home to New Jersey and donated all of their winnings to the St. Jude Children's Research Hospital.

The Bzdewkas were content to return to the family business. But thanks to *Cupcake Wars*, House of Cupcakes exploded in popularity. People piled into the bakery daily, traveling from all over. Over the next five years, business was great. Then, in the early fall of 2014, Ron got a call on his cellphone at 1:30 a.m. from the Princeton Police. The shop had caught on fire, leaving the kitchen completely charred and destroyed. Though it pained them to bid farewell to their original location, within a month they had moved one door down into a space nearly double the size.

KEEP ON TRUCKIN'

Then, in June 2015, the Bzdewka family purchased their first food truck. It wasn't long before House of Cupcakes was attending everything from seafood and barbecue festivals to street fairs and farmers' markets. They even offer catering options for any occasion.

Now, House of Cupcakes proudly operates out of four locations in Princeton, East Brunswick and Clifton, New Jersey, as well as Jeddah, Saudi Arabia. Each one offers an amazing assortment of cupcakes, with about sixty flavors in rotation at a time. In addition, they serve ice cream, cookies, edible cookie dough, chocolate-covered pretzels, cookies and crackers. They will even design and prepare custom items, from full-sized cakes and gourmet cookies to, of course, cupcakes.

House of Cupcakes keeps a mix of favorites and seasonal items on the truck. Standard choices include vanilla filled, chocolate, red velvet and chocolate chip cookie dough. Meanwhile, seasonal options include caramel apple and pumpkin spice in the fall. They often carry edible cookie dough and gourmet cookies on the truck, along with a selection of beverages such as regular and iced coffee, fresh-brewed tea, hot chocolate and apple cider.

House of Cupcakes' signature items are dense and flavorful, striking the perfect balance between sweet and satisfying. Whether they are in the bakery or on the truck, all of their cupcakes are held to the same standard and made fresh each day. Despite the ups and downs of owning a business, the Bzdewkas love what they do and are grateful to share their desserts with families across New Jersey.

Q&A with Owner Ron Bzdewka and Son Rage Bzdewka

What's the history behind House of Cupcakes?

Ron: We owned two Party Citys around fourteen years ago and eventually sold them back to the company. Soon after that, my wife had gone to a kids' event and was intrigued by all these different cupcakes. She had been baking all her life and said to me, "Hey, we should do something like that." And I said, "All right, let's try it."

Rage: She came down; she found a spot, and the next day we were in the building.

What did you do before Party City?

Ron: I was a teacher at the Middlesex County Vocational School. I was a special needs teacher, and my wife was going to hair dressing school at the same school I was teaching at. So that's where we met. I taught for seven years before I left, and we started Party City.

What was your experience like on Cupcake Wars?

Ron: It was crazy. It was so much fun! It was the real deal. And we won, and the next thing we knew, we were back on the plane—because it was filmed in California—and we're looking at each other like, "Wow, I can't believe we just won. I wonder what that means" [laughs]. But then we

couldn't tell anyone for a couple of months before it aired. Even our kids, we couldn't tell them.

The next day (after the episode aired), business exploded, and it never stopped. Sometimes people will even drive *two hours* to come here. I think that [show] is a major part of why we're still here today.

Rage: Mom wanted to keep busy. She got more than she bargained for [laughs].

What were your future experiences on the show like?

Ron: So we were on it about four times. They invited us back a few times. They were all crazy. They present you with different stuff and they throw in crazy ingredients; it's fun, but you know, you have to wing it. It was always a lot of fun for us. My wife and I went out there every time, and we had a good time. It was a blast.

You've said food truck owners who frequently attend the same events become like family. Can you describe that?

Rage: They're all great people, and so you'll go around and say hi to everyone and ask how everything has been.

Ron: Yeah, we're all very friendly with each other. So, say someone runs out of forks or napkins, you don't ever really run out, because there are a lot of other trucks you can go get the stuff from. Everybody is willing to help each other out. If someone's generator goes, everyone's got cords running from theirs to get their power going. You meet a lot of really nice people.

What are your fan-favorite cupcakes that you often bring with you to events?

Ron: Our most popular, I'd say, is the peanut butter cup. That's definitely number one. What do you think is number two, Rage?

Rage: Vanilla-filled. Kids *love* that one.

Ron: Yes, and red velvet has to be up there, too.

Rage: Red velvet, chocolate, chocolate chip cookie dough.

CHAPTER 9

MADDALENA'S
CHEESECAKE & CATERING

Frozen Chookie Cookie

1 ½ pounds butter
1 ⅛ pounds sugar
1 pound brown sugar
1 ¾ pounds flour
1 ¼ pounds graham cracker crumbs
16 eggs
4 teaspoons vanilla
2 teaspoons salt
2 teaspoons baking soda
3 pounds of 10,000-count chocolate chips

Preheat oven to 350 degrees Fahrenheit.

Cream butter. Add sugar and mix until combined.

Blend in remaining ingredients except the chocolate chips. When ingredients are blended, add chocolate chips until incorporated. Do not overmix.

Divide dough into four equal parts.

Flour tabletop generously and roll until the dough is the thickness of the chocolate chips (approximately ⅛ inch). If cookies stick, use more flour on table. Cut with cookie cutter approximately 4 inches by 4 inches.

Use baking paper on a cookie sheet and place cookies ½ inch apart. Bake in oven for 10 minutes, until light brown. Let cool for a few minutes before serving.

For an authentic Chookie, use Maddalena's CheeseCake: Let Chookie Cookie cool for at least 20 minutes after removing from oven.

Place room-temperature cheesecake in a pastry bag with a large star tip. (Alternatively, fill plastic resealable bag with cheesecake and cut a small tip from a corner.)

Flip half the cookies and pipe cheesecake onto flipped cookies. When half of the cookies are filled, top each with the remaining cookies.

Keep frozen until ready to serve.

A Strong Foundation

Eugene "Gene" Maddalena was a lifelong New Jerseyan. He was born and raised in Hunterdon County, graduating from Hunterdon Central High School in 1974. As a sophomore, he had already been accepted to the Culinary Institute of America in Hyde Park, New York. After culinary school, Gene spent the following years working his way up to banquet and executive chef positions at several distinguished New York and New Jersey restaurants.

Gene met his eventual wife Janet in the summer of 1977, when he was assistant chef at Fiddler's Elbow Country Club in Bedminster, Somerset County.

Janet took an immediate interest in Gene. But shortly after the summer season was over, Gene took a job at the Albany Country Club in New York. And when Janet returned to Fiddler's Elbow the following summer, Gene was gone.

Gene next returned to New Jersey to join a team of talented chefs in the test kitchen as they made preparations to open the East Brunswick Chateau. He and Janet soon reconnected and began dating. They married in 1980. Immediately after the couple returned from their honeymoon, they dove headfirst into the food industry to learn everything they could. Gene never wanted to own a restaurant. Though he always envisioned owning his own business, catering appealed to him more than a traditional brick-and-mortar.

In 1982, Gene and Janet founded their own catering company, offering complete event planning and catering services. It was a very labor-intensive business for the young owners, built around catering and their signature homemade Bundt-style cheesecake. The dessert proved so popular it would soon be available in local restaurants and supermarkets. The cheesecake was intended to help with cash flow while they built up their catering business, but its popularity quickly blew up. To top it off, tiered wedding cheesecakes became wildly popular in the early to mid-1980s. Just like that, their cheesecakes were in demand.

NEW BEGINNINGS

After their first year in business, the couple moved to a rural stretch of Route 31 in Ringoes and started a family. Sons Gene Jr. and Jeff started helping in the kitchen from an early age, climbing atop overturned milk crates to reach the kitchen counter as they cracked eggs and set cheesecake pans. As they grew, so did their responsibilities. They honed their culinary skills until they could bake the cheesecakes themselves. But keeping up with the intense baking and catering schedule, executing full-service catering jobs and fulfilling constant cheesecake orders was challenging for the teenage boys, who would have much preferred to be spending those weekends having fun with friends.

It was time to grow the staff, and Gene was in desperate need of a talented baker with the skills to put out one thousand or more cheesecakes per day. Trusting his gut, he took a chance and hired an inexperienced nineteen-year-old named Matt Miller.

Matt would become invaluable to Janet in the future.

Gene and Janet then took their next big risk, deciding to pursue wholesale box stores. But the high-volume demands were too much for the small family business. The challenges crippled the company, and Maddalena's was

Maddalena's fortieth-anniversary celebration.

forced to file bankruptcy. Thankfully, the family had the support of their first landlords, Sam and Dick Stofhoff. Within a year, the Stothoffs bought the property and made it possible for Maddalena's to start up again. It didn't take long for the company to regain its legs. The company continued strong for years, but another obstacle was just around the corner.

In 2001, Gene was diagnosed with cancer. As Gene Jr. and Jeff struggled with their dad's declining health, they stepped into their dad's role. With the help of Chef Scott Bevis, the small team worked long hours and managed to keep production stable while continuing to cater events. In October 2009, after a near-decade-long battle with cancer, Gene passed away in his Hunterdon County home, surrounded by loved ones. Janet, Gene Jr., Jeff and Scott were all by his bedside.

Since Gene's passing, Maddalena's has proudly carried on his legacy. They continue to be among New Jersey's top cheesecake providers and a beloved Hunterdon County namesake.

MADDALENA'S LIVES ON

In 2014, the family warmly welcomed Matt Miller back to the business after nearly twenty years. The team describes it as a blessing to have him back, and Janet and her sons believe Gene Sr. had a hand in Matt's return. They built a mobile dessert truck and expanded their menu to include cheesecake on a stick. It wasn't long before they added three more mobile units and were spending their weekends at festivals and wineries all over New Jersey.

By 2018, they had expanded their menu to include gluten-free and keto cheesecakes at their storefront, as well as frozen cheesecakes that can be thawed and eaten at a later date. They also offer apple crumb pie and their signature Chookie, the result of sandwiching Maddalena's cheesecake between two graham cracker/chocolate chip cookies. The Chookie is one of several dessert options Maddalena's also offers from their truck, which first hit the road in 2014. Other popular items include cheesecake slices and cheesecake-filled cannoli—both served on a stick! Plus, any of those three options can be dipped in chocolate and covered in toppings like sprinkles, graham cracker crumbs, homemade chocolate chip cookie or peanut butter cookie crumbs, mixed nuts, toasted coconut or even bacon bits.

Maddalena's CheeseCake celebrated its forty-year anniversary in 2022. They're an enduring brand that has withstood decades of changes and challenges. They've made it through bankruptcy, a recession, loss, food shortages and, most recently, the COVID-19 pandemic. The name Maddalena's exemplifies resiliency and perseverance, persisting through trials and tribulations to deliver the best frozen cheesecake New Jersey has to offer.

"When you take a bite of Gene's cheesecake or his apple crumb pie, I know we are sharing a little bit of Gene's spirit, and he will never be forgotten," Janet says.

Q&A with Co-Founder Janet Maddalena

You and your husband, Gene, started Maddalena's back in 1982. Tell us about the evolution from 1982 to now.
We've been through a lot. We've done a lot. Cheesecake was supposed to be sort of a little side gig while we built up our catering business, and as we've gotten older, we've focused much more on cheesecake.

The most important thing is the recipe is the same, the quality is the same; but we've done so many new things with it.

Gene kept continuously working through the years. What different roles did he play in the business?
He did a little bit of everything. Back in the day, Gene would start at one o'clock in the morning; he would go out and start mixing the batters. So he was splitting himself so many different ways, and he was such a shining star. He was a really special kind of guy with a special energy. He had a smile as big as you could imagine. And he was loved by everybody.

What made you open your storefront in Ringoes?
We thought it would be a great, simple way to sell some of our products. We really enjoy catering, and it's a big part of Maddalena's; but how many people who book you for a party of a hundred people do that every month or year? Sometimes it's a once-in-a-lifetime event. What we're doing with the store is we're building on the elements of our business that our customers love.

At the store, guests can get a number of dessert and food items without everything else that comes with catering; it's easy for them to just stop in and grab a cheesecake or chicken potpie or something else.

What are your most popular types of cheesecakes?

Vanilla is always the most popular. It's the original. Most people just say, "I want plain." So that's the most popular of our flavors.

Black Forest has also become very popular. It's cherries swirled into vanilla cheesecake in a pan that's been layered with chocolate crumbs. So that's a nice one, too. We also do red velvet cheesecake.

What made you start the food truck?

When Gene died in 2009, the world was going through a tough time—the economy just was not good. And the boys, my sons Jeff and Gene, and I talked about if we should keep the business going. I think because this is all we've ever done; my sons were born here on this property, and this was their world and *mine*.

If I was really thinking, I probably would have just said it's a good time to put it to bed; but for some reason, we couldn't do that. I had trouble doing it, mostly because I thought we should finish what he started—what he was unable to do. So a few years ago, we began the food truck part of our business.

What items can customers get off your truck?

Cheesecake on a stick, and then we dip it in chocolate. We make our own chocolate chip cookies and our own peanut butter cookies, and then we toast them and turn them into toppings. We have sprinkles, and we'll do coconut toasted, and we also have Oreo cookie crumbs and mixed nuts.

We have the Chookie on the truck and the cheesecake-filled cannoli, which can also be dipped and topped. In addition, we also make a phenomenal apple crumb pie. We do apple pie à la mode on the truck. And then we make the cheesecake gelato, and we usually have about four or five different flavors on the truck.

Additionally, we always have iced coffee and limeade on the truck. It's simple, but it goes along great with what we offer.

So what items do you see flying out of your truck when you're at events?

Cheesecake on a stick outsells everything. But sometimes, the warm apple pie we can't keep up with, especially if it's a cooler day. Then toppings popularity is funny, because one day everybody wants peanut butter, and then the next day everybody wants coconut.

CHAPTER 10
THE MEXI-BOYS

Pico de Gallo

1 pound tomatoes, chopped
½ onion (approximately 1 cup), chopped
½ cup cilantro, chopped
½ yellow pepper, chopped
1 lime, juiced
½ teaspoon salt
⅛ teaspoon black pepper

Dice tomatoes, onion, cilantro and yellow pepper. Then combine in medium bowl. Stir in lime juice and lightly season with salt and black pepper. (Can add more or less depending on preference.)

Salsa Verde

1 ¾ pounds tomatillos (around 15 medium), husked and rinsed
1 medium jalapeño, no stem
½ cup white onion, chopped
⅓ cup packed fresh cilantro leaves
1 tablespoon lime juice, freshly squeezed
1 teaspoon salt

Place the tomatillos and jalapeño in a frying pan and use low heat until they are black in some areas. Try to keep turning them to get an even cook all around. Normally takes 5 to 10 minutes.

In a blender, add the chopped onion, cilantro, lime juice and salt. Blend for 1 minute.

Remove the tomatillos and jalapeño from the frying pan and add to blender. Blend until reaching desired consistency. (More lime juice or salt can be added to reach desired flavor.)

~~~

A Taste of Mexico

Eduardo Rojas and Alex Sanchez were food truckers before they were food truckers. To clarify, their food trucking journey began several years before the Mexi-Boys was founded.

Eduardo was born to Mexican immigrants and raised in Highland Park, New Jersey. Growing up, his parents introduced him to the vibrant culture and zesty, absorbing cuisine of his Mexican heritage. While living in the United States, the family re-created traditional Mexican dishes, encouraging Eduardo to put his own creative spin on authentic meals.

Meanwhile, Alex was born in Puebla, Mexico. The city, just southeast of Mexico City, is known for its food and art. Specifically, Puebla birthed a number of sauces and dishes that are recognized and re-created internationally, including mole poblano, chiles en nogada and the cemita. The latter is a sandwich stuffed with beef, pork, chicken, cheeses and an array of fresh peppers and seasonings.

Left to right: Fried shrimp tacos and taquitos.

After graduating from Kean University with a degree in business management, Eduardo began a career in the food industry. He currently serves as the director of operations for a food company. He eventually connected with a food truck owner and also began working on his truck, where he met Alex (another employee on the truck). The fast friends shared a similar work ethic and an equally strong desire to start their own business. Soon after, Eduardo and Alex left their previous food truck jobs and set off on their own.

WALK BEFORE YOU RUN

But before starting a food truck, the Mexi-Boys took a scaled-down approach, attending events with tables and a tent. Despite their humble beginnings, much of the menu remains the same; including the signature Mexi-Boys fried burrito, which is *not* to be confused with a chimichanga! Eduardo comically compares their fried burrito to what would happen if an empanada and a burrito had a baby.

Two years after founding the Mexi-Boys, Eduardo and Alex bought their first truck. They debuted in the fall of 2020 and within a year expanded to a second truck. Beyond the fried burrito, the Mexi-Boys offer a selection of taquitos, tamales and quesadillas. They also offer bowls and loaded nachos. Eduardo and Alex source fresh ingredients and craft their recipes to ensure that every bite is loaded with flavor.

The Mexi-Boys serves both traditional Mexican cuisine as well as vegan twists on their classic dishes. Eduardo and Alex spent years cooking for family and friends, and they bring the same passion to their food truck. By sharing their cuisine with patrons across New Jersey, New York and Pennsylvania, Eduardo and Alex are also sharing their Mexican background and traditions.

Eventgoers who spot the Mexi-Boys trucks at an event or party can rest assured that either Eduardo or Alex is in command. It's an even bigger treat when both of them are on hand, laughing and joking on the opposite side of the window. One could say the Mexi-Boys has been generations in the making. Now they've arrived and deliver an unparalleled food trucking experience.

Q&A with Co-Owner Eduardo Rojas

What made you want to start a food truck?

The both of us had a passion for the business and saw the hard work it took. If you know us, we don't shy away from hard work. One day, we realized we wanted to try to start our own business. We started in 2018 with a tent and a whole lot of ideas. At the end of 2020, we were fortunate enough to purchase our first truck, and at the end of 2021, we bought our second.

How did you come up with your concept?

Our hero product is the fried burrito. We wanted something that can be handheld but bring a ton of flavor in the first bite. We also wanted something that could be a quick-serve item and an instant favorite. And yes, it's almost like a chimichanga, but it's the Mexi-Boys version of a chimichanga, which makes it a million times better. A chimichanga is a full-size burrito that is fried.

We are a Mexican food truck that wanted to stand out. We wanted to stand out not only with our flavor but also in the appearance of our food. Our concept is constantly evolving.

What sets your food truck apart?

We pride ourselves on the flavor of our food. I think it really comes out when you taste our food. We are trying to share the experience of our version of Mexican food with our customers.

What type of menu items do you offer off the truck?

We have both traditional Mexican food and a menu with vegan twists on our classic dishes. On our menu, you can find traditional offerings like tacos, tamales and quesadillas, as well as items like fried burritos, the Mexi-Boys Cone and Mexi fries. We top everything with our homemade salsa verde and pico de gallo.

What are some of your most popular menu items?

Fried burritos, taquitos and quesadillas. The Mexi bowl and the loaded nachos are also crowd favorites.

What types of catering options do you offer?

We offer catering options for any kind of need. Corporate, birthdays, weddings and other events.

How much have you learned food trucking over the years?
You have to have a long-term financial mindset and a short-term memory when it comes to challenges that come up.

At the end of the day, a food truck is a business. Like any business, you have to properly manage it financially in order to sustain it. An owner has to develop a short-term memory when it comes to issues that come up. Fix the issue, use the lessons learned and move forward. It's also important to put a process or a plan of action in place to help avoid it from happening again. The biggest thing Alex and I have learned is that there is nothing better than owning your own trucks!

PART III

· ·

JERSEY SHORE FOOD TRUCKS

· ·

11. Five Sisters Food Co.
Recipe: Surf N Turf Burger
Biography
Q&A with Owner George Miller and Daughter Ashley Miller

12. Jersey Roll
Recipe: Pork Roll, Egg and Cheese Sandwich
Biography
Q&A with Co-Founder John Fels

13. Ohana Food Truck
Recipe: Braised Short Ribs with Asian Slaw and Chili Aioli
Recipe: Ceviche with Fresh Tortilla Chips
Biography
Q&A with Partners Matthew Smith, Gavin DeCapua, Candy Blake,
Dana Costello and James Costello

14. Shore Good Eats 'N' Treats
Recipe: Apple Pie Egg Rolls
Recipe: Buffalo Chicken Egg Rolls
Biography
Q&A with Co-Founder Steve Fahnholz

15. Kiersten's Creations
Recipe: Key Lime Pops
Recipe: Peanut Butter Pie
Biography
Q&A with Owner Kiersten Connor

CHAPTER II

FIVE SISTERS FOOD CO.

Surf N Turf Burger

One of the best things about burgers (other than how delicious they are) is their versatility and the amount of flavor combinations you can make with them. The next time you're going to make burgers, try topping them with this jumbo lump crab dip and Sriracha tartar sauce recipe. Why have a plain old burger when you can take a quick weeknight grilled burger and elevate it with just a few ingredients?

— Libby Miller

Crab Dip

8 ounces cream cheese, softened
½ cup mayonnaise
1 tablespoon lemon juice
¼ tablespoon Sriracha
3 green onions, finely chopped
3 tablespoons Parmesan
½ teaspoon Old Bay Seasoning
12 ounces lump crab

Sriracha Tartar Sauce

½ cup mayonnaise

1 ½ tablespoons lemon juice (from about ¼ lemon)
1 ½ tablespoons Sriracha
¼ teaspoon kosher salt
⅛ teaspoon freshly ground black pepper

Burger
4 (8-ounce) Angus beef patties
1 teaspoon Old Bay Seasoning
4 brioche hamburger rolls

Crab Dip: In a medium-sized bowl, mix softened cream cheese, mayonnaise, lemon juice, Sriracha, chopped green onions, Parmesan and Old Bay Seasoning. Fold in crab meat and refrigerate until needed.

Tartar Sauce: In a separate bowl, mix mayonnaise, lemon juice, Sriracha, salt and ground black pepper. Stir to blend. Cover and refrigerate until needed. (May be stored for up to one day.)

Burger: Season burger patties with Old Bay Seasoning and grill.

When cooked to desired temperature, remove burgers from grill and place on brioche roll. Top with desired amount of crab dip and Sriracha tartar sauce and enjoy!

~~~

THE SISTERHOOD OF THE TRAVELING TRUCK

Ashley, Hailey, Summer, Savannah and Piper are the five sisters who make up…well, Five Sisters Food Co. Theirs are the bright, smiling faces who greet you at the window, help to prepare your order and hand you your radiant boats of burgers and sandwiches. Along with their mother, Libby, and father, George, the Miller family own and operate a premier Garden State food truck.

Five Sisters Food Co. was born in 2010 as a catering company run by Libby. Though there may be some slight bias, she is proclaimed the best cook by each one of her daughters, so catering was always an obvious career choice.

"Whenever we'd go out to eat, she'd always come home and make the meals better than the actual restaurant," her oldest daughter, Ashley, recalls with a laugh. "It's crazy, because she can just taste something and then go home and whip it up—no recipe or anything."

After launching their website, the catering company immediately booked clients for every weekend. George, a Perth Amboy firefighter by day, even contributed to the business. He added his own smoked pork to the menu, as well as a fleet of two food trucks. The first of the two hit the road in 2014. In the beginning, it was just Libby, George and their two oldest daughters: Ashley at fifteen and Hailey at twelve.

Throughout the following eight years, the remaining sisters joined the ranks, one by one. These days, you will find all five running the show at events—with only *some* assistance from Mom and Dad. Each station is handled with a blazing dexterity and vigilant attentiveness. It's an impressive operation, made only more remarkable by the food they consistently produce.

FIVE SISTERS, COUNTLESS COWS

Five Sisters is known for their burgers, but the truck offers a somewhat-rotating menu. In particular, the burger options range from your more traditional Mac Daddy (two Angus burgers with American cheese, bacon, mac and cheese bites and their signature BBQ sauce) to the exclusive Pork Belly (two slow-braised teriyaki pork belly slices with fresh cucumber, Asian slaw and garlic aioli). Meanwhile, their Whiskey Tango includes two whiskey-glazed burgers topped with thick-cut Applewood smoked bacon, aged cheddar, onion petals and their own bourbon barbecue sauce. The Jersey has two Angus burgers topped with thick-cut applewood-smoked bacon, onion petals, American cheese, fried pickles, fries and Five Sisters' "awesome sauce." Other favorites include the creamy Brie burger, the Smokehouse burger, the Moonshine, burger No. 7, the Pig Mac and, another popular favorite, the Surf N Turf burger.

Beyond the burgers, Five Sisters occasionally offers some of my favorite fat sandwiches. Made popular by the Rutgers University grease trucks, the Miller family has turned a swelling sandwich into a gourmet handheld meal. (You could even argue it's big enough for *two* meals.) Packed thick, the fat sandwiches come with a selection of innards. The Philly comes with cheesesteak, chicken fingers, mozzarella sticks and fries, all in a hoagie roll, whereas the Buffalo includes chicken cheesesteak, chicken fingers, mozzarella sticks, buffalo sauce, ranch and fries.

As for sides, they offer Pig Fries topped with pulled pork and a Mac N Cheese Cone, which is four-cheese mac and cheese topped with barbecue bacon jam and served in a waffle cone.

The Millers mostly focus on the truck, but they still welcome catering for large private events. When the business first started, they would go all out: tables, chairs, service and everything in between. But in the years since, catering has become more of a special event. The Miller family will drive up to your location in their chrome-and-charcoal-studded truck, "Five Sisters Food Co." proudly displayed from all angles. They offer their full menu and are a great choice to enhance those corporate lunches, wedding after-parties and other social gatherings.

Family Bonding

While Libby is the mastermind behind the menu, her daughters and husband help to execute the items on the trucks. You could say that Five Sisters has nailed the art of acquiring cheap labor. In all seriousness, they've raised the bar for what it means to be a family business. Five Sisters Food Co. produces some of the best burgers, sliders and sandwiches in the *nation*, let alone the state of New Jersey, and they've accomplished everything through the support and commitment of the entire family.

Nearly a decade with the trucks has allowed the Miller clan to stay connected in ways that a lot of large families miss out on. They've also learned skills—teamwork, communication, problem solving—that help to strengthen those bonds. As parents, Libby and George are watching their young girls grow, persevere and learn right before their eyes. Food trucking presents its share of challenges from which Five Sisters is not exempt. However, it's during those times that familial support—as well as the camaraderie of the food truck community—is invaluable.

I've visited the truck numerous times over the years and am perpetually impressed by how smoothly the family operates together. My brothers and I can't even carpool to a movie without throwing jabs and squabbling about the radio. The Miller sisters, on the other hand, always have smiles on their faces and a constant reinforcement of one another. I'm sure there's the occasional argument here and there, but nothing that disrupts their fluid teamwork. The first time I spoke to Ashley, she complimented her sisters and the significant roles they each play in the business. Their laughs and smiles only grow as the events pick up and the lines deepen; they simply get down to business, heads forward, voices steady, all five working together.

Q&A WITH OWNER GEORGE MILLER AND DAUGHTER ASHLEY MILLER

How did your mom get into catering?

George Miller: Libby would always cook, and once the kids got older, we thought, "Hey, why don't we start a catering business?" We partnered up with a local restaurant, and we used their kitchen.

Ashley: She made a website, and as soon as it launched, we were booked every weekend basically all year round. Then one summer, my dad bought a smoker, and we started doing pig roasts. That business was called iPigRoast. Then that winter, we found a food truck on Craigslist.

What are some specialty items that the truck offers?

Ashley: We have this five-cheese mac and cheese inside a waffle cone, and my mom makes this applewood-smoked bacon barbecue jam, and that's put on top. We also have fries with jumbo lump crab dip, and we load it up with pulled pork.

We also get pork belly on our truck every once in a while. It's essentially what bacon is made out of, but it's a thick slab of it, and we slow roast it; then my mom makes garlic aioli and Asian slaw dressing. All of the ingredients melt together and melt in your mouth. We won a bunch of awards for that, so it's one of the more popular items we offer; but it's really hard to get. We purchase it from a German butcher, and he doesn't have it all the time.

What is your most popular menu item?

Ashley: I would say the pork belly when we have it, but also the Whiskey Tango Sliders. We actually won best burger truck in America for that. It's a cheddar cheeseburger with bacon, whiskey glaze, bourbon barbecue sauce and a fried onion blossom on top. That's my favorite too. I eat it almost every day, and I've been working here for years. I can never get sick of it [laughs].

Do you remember your first event with the truck?

George: One of our first shows was at Laurita Winery. It was me, Libby, Ashley and Hailey—my two older girls—and Ashley was fifteen…

Ashley: And Hailey was twelve, and she was on the fryer at twelve years old [laughs].

George: [Laughs]. We didn't know what to expect. We got to Laurita and opened up, and there was a line all the way up the path. But we did it.

Ashley: Yeah, we learned throughout the years—what worked, what didn't.

George: We're still learning stuff. The nice thing with the truck is that it keeps us all together, and that's what I like about it. I'm a firefighter up north, and I'll be gone for a couple days a week, and I don't get to see everyone. But it's nice with the truck that we're all together. We get to see different venues and meet new people.

CHAPTER 12

JERSEY ROLL

Pork Roll, Egg and Cheese Sandwich

3 tablespoons butter
4 to 5 slices pork roll
2 large eggs
Kosher salt and ground black pepper
Kaiser roll
2 slices American cheese

Heat a flattop grill or nonstick skillet over medium-high heat. Add 2 tablespoons of butter to surface.

Heat a separate pan to medium-low heat and add the other tablespoon of butter.

When butter melts, place all pork roll slices on the first pan. Score the edges of the pork roll in four places each. Leave in pan for several minutes, until underside is just browned. Then flip pork roll slices.

In the other pan, crack 2 eggs. Discard the shells. After a couple minutes, season eggs with salt and pepper, then flip.

Cut your Kaiser roll in half and pile the bottom slice with pork roll, cheese and eggs, alternating between each. Then cover with top bun and serve.

~~~

Birds of a Feather

There's an age-old debate in New Jersey about whether one of the state's signature meats is called Taylor ham or pork roll. That debate can now be put to rest, because it's called pork roll. Taylor ham is as imaginary as the Jersey Devil supposedly running around the Pine Barrens. (Actually, it might be *more* imaginary than the Jersey Devil.) The brand Taylor even calls it pork roll on its packaging. If that's not enough evidence, just ask John Fels and Bobby O'Donnell, two lifelong New Jersey residents and entrepreneurs who built their entire business around the food.

John and Bobby grew up in Jackson Township. They attended elementary, middle and even high school together. There paths didn't diverge until high school graduation; John enrolled at Rider University, while Bobby went to Ocean County College for a bit before starting his own construction business. While in college, John started his own landscaping business based out of the Ocean County area and continued to build it up after graduating.

Even during the time they were apart, John and Bobby remained friends. As adults, they went out as a group, taking their wives to food truck events throughout the state. Admiring the vast cuisines, relaxed atmosphere and fun themes, the two developed a desire to be part of the food trucking scene. But they didn't know what they wanted to sell.

GET PIGGY WITH IT

It didn't take long to settle on pork roll, something both men ate every day. They figured the Garden State staple would draw a crowd, and they were right. During Jersey Roll's inaugural event in 2017, they garnered long lines and satisfied customers. Though the first year proved a challenge—John and Bobby juggled responsibilities on the truck with full-time jobs—Jersey Roll experienced a lot of success. So much so, in fact, that they opened a storefront the following year.

The Jersey Roll brick-and-mortar debuted in the spring of 2018, right on the Seaside Heights boardwalk. Given the shore town's warm-weather appeal, the shop is open annually from spring through fall. Though many truck favorites appear on the menu, the Jersey Roll storefront expands the menu even more. In particular, they offer about a dozen different selections and specials.

Signature items include the Dirty Bow Tie: a mozzarella stick wrapped in a deep-fried slice of breaded pork roll and tied with a strip of bacon. They also have a burger, breaded wings and even a pork roll sandwich with pineapples and barbecue sauce. Of course, they serve the classic pork roll, egg and cheese on a Kaiser, aptly named Pig and a Yolk.

More Trucks, More Bucks

The Jersey Roll shop is always evolving its menu, but working on the truck is still John and Bobby's greatest passion. In 2019, the duo expanded to include a second truck. John manages one as Bobby manages the other, covering twice as many events per season. In addition to festivals and events, they offer several different catering packages for parties, corporate functions and more.

Since the beginning of their enterprise, John and Bobby have operated under the slogan "Keeping a great tradition Jersey Strong." In the years since, the two friends have founded an enduring brand that celebrates a New Jersey staple, bringing patrons together as a community through a shared love of a classic food. One that is *definitely* called pork roll and not Taylor ham.

Q&A with Co-Founder John Fels

What is the draw of pork roll? Why do so many New Jerseyans find it so tantalizing?

It's the taste. And the flavor. It's everything that you want in the morning. Where bacon sometimes is a little too much of one thing, pork roll is a little bit of that *something*; and it's easy to eat in the morning. It pairs awesome with egg and cheese. And we've just taken that to a whole other level now with the sandwiches we make.

What types of items do you offer on the truck?

We have the standard pork roll egg and cheese; then we came up with a breaded pork roll with melted provolone and marinara called the Dirty Italian. We do loaded tots—we call it Dirty Pig—which is tater tots topped with melted cheese and pieces of pork roll. Then we do a Jersey Burger,

Asian Slaw: In a large pan, add 2 bags of slaw mix. Add in rice wine vinegar, fish sauce and soy sauce.

Thinly slice red and green bell peppers long ways. Add peppers to pan.

Add sesame oil and sesame seeds.

Mix well.

Chili Aioli: Mix sour cream, mayonnaise, sambal oelek, salt, pepper and lemon juice together well until all ingredients are incorporated.

Serve Braised Short Rib with side of Asian Slaw and Chili Aioli. Enjoy!

Ceviche with Fresh Tortilla Chips

Ceviche
1 gallon vegetable or canola oil
1 red pepper
1 yellow pepper
1 small red onion
4 ounces mango
4 ounces pineapple
1 jalapeño
8 ounces sushi-grade tuna
2 ounces lemon juice or yuzu
Salt and pepper to taste

Tortilla Chips
10 (6-inch) flour tortillas
Oil for frying
Salt

Ceviche: In a large pot, heat oil to 375 degrees or a slight rolling boil.

Dice peppers, onion, mango, pineapple and jalapeño.

In a separate bowl, dice tuna and add lemon juice. Let sit for 30 seconds.

Combine pepper/onion/fruit/jalapeño with tuna.
Add a pinch of salt and pepper. Toss entire mix with a spoon.

Tortilla Chips: If making fresh chips, cut flour tortilla in six equal pieces.
Place a handful of chips in oil.

Use tongs to turn chips over so they brown evenly.

Once browned, take out of oil with slotted spoon and toss in a bowl
with a pinch of salt.

Serve and enjoy!

OHANA MEANS FAMILY

When New Jersey teachers get together, no idea is off-limits. That includes
going all-in together on a food truck.

Dana Costello grew up working on the Jersey Shore. During most of the
year, she taught at Toms River High School South, but her summers were

dedicated to the Blue Water Grill restaurant, where she connected with the clientele, jived with her coworkers and enjoyed every bit of the cuisine. In 2010, the owner informed Dana that they were looking to sell. In that moment, Dana knew exactly what she wanted. Dana and her husband, James, closed on the restaurant at the end of 2010. One year, a fresh menu and a few renovations later, Ohana Grill was born.

James, who had been down the shore since 1984, had spent most of his career in the bar business. He worked his way up from a bartender to bar owner. Throughout Ohana's first year, James worked in the kitchen under two experienced chefs. James had experience in the kitchen, but he maintains that the education and skills he learned from these two chefs are invaluable. After both men left Ohana, James took over the kitchen, which he has been leading for the past decade.

Candy Blake and Gavin DeCapua—also from Toms River High School South—and Matthew Smith from Toms River Intermediate School spent nearly a decade sporting various hats at Ohana Grill. Mostly serving and hosting, the three spent many of their summers at the restaurant, learning the ins and outs of the food industry. Then one evening out together, as the bar tab grew, they had an idea: how about starting a food truck? It was only a thought—a small spark—but by the next morning, the spark had caught fire, and Dana, James, Candy, Gavin and Matthew set their plans in motion.

A MENU FOR EVERY MEAL

The group purchased their food truck midway through the 2019 season, debuting at Laurita Winery in August of the same year. The five knew that Laurita's events were revered and that countless foodies would be lining up at their window from early in the day until the end of the night. By the end of the event, they had a following. The trend continued throughout every subsequent event Ohana attended. Even when they changed up their menu, everything seemed to be a hit. Just like in his restaurant, James enjoyed trying new recipes, working with different ingredients, seeing what specials he could create for different food truck events.

Ohana Food Truck offers just about everything. The menu rotates so that no two events are identical, but fan favorites return often. Among their most popular dishes is the warm lobster roll and fries, consisting of a round Hawaiian roll packed with fresh Maine lobster and topped carefully with

Left to right: Fresh tortilla chips with ceviche and braised short rib tacos.

butter. Other Ohana hits include their selection of tacos served on flour tortillas. The braised short rib tacos are topped with James's signature Asian slaw and chili aioli. Meanwhile, the blackened shrimp tacos and crispy fish tacos are crowned with iceberg lettuce and chili aioli, with an extra helping of corn bean salsa on the fish tacos. They occasionally do pork roll sandwiches, chicken fingers and even a cheeseburger taco. Depending on the event and occasion, Ohana can fluidly alternate between breakfast, lunch and dinner fare.

Ohana offers a taste of Hawaii in Lavallette, New Jersey. Its cuisine may not be black and white, but James and his team never fail to provide a fusion of flavors. The truck, once an extension of the brick-and-mortar, has become its own entity in recent years. Ohana Food Truck is not bound by the restaurant's specials; it's not restricted to its counterpart's menu. James, Dana, Candy, Gavin and Matthew are happy to give the food truck a life of its own. The truck's dynamic menu and flexible cuisine have enabled the rig to fit in wherever it's called.

Q&A with Partners Matthew Smith, Gavin DeCapua, Candy Blake, Dana Costello and James Costello

Tell us about yourselves.

Matthew Smith: I grew up in Lavallette, and I worked as a teacher, which was how I was able to get some information about becoming a server here at the restaurant [Ohana Grill]. And then working here for about eight years, I became very friendly with James and Dana, who own it, and after a couple beers had an idea to start a food truck [laughs].

Gavin DeCapua: I was a teacher for thirty-two years, but in that span, I also ran summer concession food stands in Monmouth County at private beach clubs for about twenty-five years. I was getting ready to retire from teaching and spoke to Dana, and she said they were talking about starting a food truck, and I thought it would be up my alley to get involved in my retirement. I gave up the summer concession stands and decided to go with them. I retired this past June 2021. There was a little overlap with the truck—I had to make sure it was going to be a success first [laughs].

Candy Blake: I grew up in Manville. So I'm a transplant [laughs]. I moved to the area from Manville in 1986 and have been down here ever since. I moved down here for a teaching job, and I just retired as a teacher also, after thirty-six years of teaching, in October 2021. I've always been involved in food service ever since I was thirteen. I worked at the Jolly Ox in Somerset County. Dana offered me a job here at Ohana six or seven years ago, and I've been working as a server, hostess—wherever they need a fill-in. I was afforded the opportunity to go in on the truck as a partner, and I knew I was getting ready to retire, so I joined, too.

Dana Costello: I was born in Paterson but grew up in Manchester. I worked on the boardwalk since I was fourteen, so I've always loved the food business, and I worked here when it was Blue Water Grill as a server. The guy was looking to sell, and I called my husband and said, "Hi, we're buying a restaurant" [laughs]. And we bought the restaurant but wanted to do a little bit more. We always thought about doing a food truck, but it was always too much for the two of us to handle. And we talked with Candy and Gavin and Matt and decided to go all in.

James Costello: I think it started with about nine partners. And then one by one as you talk to people… [laughs].

Gavin: Dana was always gung-ho about it. She was *persistent*.

Dana: A lot of us talked about it one night, and then the next day when there was some clarity and we realized it was coming to fruition, it was left with us five.

James: I grew up in Jersey City. I moved down the shore in 1984. Always worked on the boardwalk. That's where me and Dana met. But I was mostly in the bar business most of my life—bartender, bar manager, bar owner. And then I was running a bar and restaurant for a friend of mine, and then Dana called about this proposition, and I quit my corporate job and bought Ohana. I have pretty much been the head chef since the first year. It seemed like a good plan that we could cook our food here for the truck and get prepared for the events.

The first year, I worked as the sous chef. I worked between one chef that was from Johnson & Wales and another chef that was from the Culinary Institute of America, and they said to me, "In one year you'll learn more from us than you would in culinary school," because I basically had two schools teaching me. And by the end of the first year, the head chef left, and I said, "I got it. No problem." I mean, I always knew how to cook, but to cook to this level you need more training. But that never ends, because everyone who comes through our kitchen teaches everybody something, and hopefully we teach them something, too.

What was your first time out like with the truck?
Matt: That was Laurita in 2019.

Candy: And I remember the first sale was French fries. I remember we were all excited: "French fries!" [laughs] We have all these great things on our menu, and what does the first person order? Side of fries and a water.

Was there much of a learning curve adjusting to the truck after years working in an established restaurant?
Candy: I think there's a big learning curve being a truck owner. I think we learned a lot in three years. We are *so improved* from where we started. At Laurita, we were the first ones in and the last ones out [laughs]. We were rookies. The food was never a problem, though.

Dana: The first night on the truck, we ran out of water washing our dishes. So you have to learn to conserve. You have to learn differently than you would in a restaurant setting.

Gavin: I always worked with grills and fryers at the beachfront. So it wasn't that much of a problem for me in the food truck with that respect. I was good with the fast food, but with the higher-end food, I just watched and learned. It took some time to learn.

Matt: The first year was a lot of working through everything—what did we need to work on with the truck, what foods, what *didn't* work on the truck. Not everything translates well from the restaurant to the truck.

Describe your cuisine.
Dana: People ask a lot, and it's difficult to exactly pin down. We often say Asian fusion. But we almost have American-Asian fusion.

James: American-Asian-Hawaiian fusion [laughs]. Hawaiian itself is Asian fusion, because most Hawaiian food comes from about four different Asian islands that all met in Hawaii and melded their food. But we also try to Americanize it and put our own spins on it.

Matt: That's what makes us popular for birthdays and parties, because we can always adapt to whatever someone's looking for. We can do anything from burgers and fries to surf and turf.

What kind of desserts can guests get from Ohana Grill?
Candy: We've done a cookie skillet that was a big seller. The desserts, everything's made here. Dana makes a cheesecake for dessert—people *love* the homemade cheesecake.

James: It all comes back in rotation though. Like, we're not doing a set dessert menu *right now*, but we'll do a rotation so that every night we could bring some new stuff in.

What is the restaurant's schedule like through the year?

Dana: Year round we're open Thursday through Saturday. But during the summer, we're open seven days a week—that's June until Labor Day.

CHAPTER 14

SHORE GOOD EATS 'N' TREATS

Apple Pie Egg Rolls

Filling
Fuji/Gala and Granny Smith apples
Butter
Brown sugar
Cinnamon
Nutmeg
Pinch of salt
Pie crust
Lemon juice

Egg Roll
Egg roll wrappers
Water
Oil (preferably canola), for frying

Filling: Core, peel and slice all apples. Preheat oven to 350 degrees Fahrenheit. Sauté apples until tender with butter and dry ingredients.

Using your favorite store-bought pie crust, place sautéed apples on top of pie crust, then cover with more crust. Vent the top pie crust.

Place pie in oven and bake until pie crust is golden brown and cooked. (Apples are already cooked.)

Remove from oven and let cool completely.

Egg Roll: Place egg roll wrapper(s) with the flour-coated side down. It should look like a diamond in front of you. Put 4 ounces of egg roll filling into the center of the wrapper. When scooping, make sure to get both apples and crust onto the egg roll wrapper. Brush water over the edges of the wrapper.

Fold the corner closest to you over the filling with your thumb and index finger and cover the filling while molding the filling into a log shape. Then, while still holding that position with your thumbs, use your index and middle fingers to fold the two side corners over the top of the corner you folded into the center until they touch.

Next, roll the egg roll forward so you no longer see the folded corners. You should then see two small corners sticking out from the wrapper and the one corner you haven't touched yet. Use your pinky fingers to fold those small corners in, and then roll the egg roll over until it completely closes over that last corner.

Fry: Heat oil to 350 degrees Fahrenheit. Gently place prepared egg rolls into fryer and let sit for approximately 3 to 4 minutes, or until golden brown and crispy on the outside. Roll in cinnamon sugar immediately upon removal from fryer. Be careful: they are HOT.

Let cool for 1 to 2 minutes, cut and serve!

Buffalo Chicken Egg Rolls

Buffalo Sauce
1 gallon hot sauce
2 pounds butter
2 tablespoons salt
2 tablespoons pepper
2 tablespoons dry parsley
3 tablespoons garlic powder
1½ cups red wine vinegar

Filling
10 pounds chicken breast
Salt
Pepper
Parsley
2½ pounds shredded cheddar jack cheese

Egg Roll
Oil (we use canola), for frying
Egg roll wrappers
Water

Buffalo Sauce: Mix hot sauce, butter, salt, pepper, parsley, garlic powder and red wine vinegar together in a large pot. Cook on medium heat until butter is melted. Simmer for 15 minutes, then cool to room temperature. (Can be stored for 4 to 6 weeks.)

Filling: Preheat oven to 350 degrees Fahrenheit. Put all 10 pounds of chicken breast on a sheet pan or baking sheet and season both sides with salt, pepper and parsley to your liking. Roast the chicken breast in the oven for 30 to 40 minutes (or until internal temperature is 165 degrees Fahrenheit).

Remove chicken from oven and let cool until it is cool enough to handle (usually 15 to 20 minutes). Cut chicken into small cubes. It will shred a little bit if it is still warm (which is good—we want that).

Place cut-up chicken into a large mixing bowl and add approximately 4 cups of your delicious buffalo sauce. Add in shredded cheddar jack cheese and mix until everything is incorporated and coated together. If the chicken and buffalo sauce are still warm, the cheese will begin to melt, which is exactly what we want.

Egg Roll: Place egg roll wrapper(s) with the flour-coated side down. It should look like a diamond in front of you. Put 4 ounces of egg roll filling into the center of the wrapper. Brush water over the edges of the wrapper.

Fold the corner closest to you over the filling with your thumb and index finger and cover the filling while molding the filling into a log shape. Then, while still holding that position with your thumbs, use your index and middle fingers to fold the two side corners over the top of the corner you folded into the center until they touch.

Roll the egg roll forward so you no longer see the folded corners. You should then see two small corners sticking out from the wrapper, and the one corner you haven't touched yet. Use your pinky fingers to fold those small corners in and roll your egg roll over until it completely closes over that last corner.

Fry: Heat oil to 350 degrees Fahrenheit. Gently place prepared egg rolls into fryer and let sit for approximately 3 to 4 minutes, or until golden brown and crispy on the outside.

Remove from fryer and let cool for 1 to 2 minutes, cut and serve!

~~~

SERVING THE COMMUNITY IN MORE WAYS THAN ONE

Steve and Natalie Fahnholz didn't know they were destined for food truck greatness. Natalie was a paraprofessional in the Jackson School District in Ocean County. During her seventeen years of service, she worked as an in-class aid for children with special needs. After she retired from her profession in December 2015, she was ready to take on a new endeavor.

Meanwhile, Steve became a first responder while still in high school. He volunteered as an EMT and a firefighter and worked as a dispatcher for the Avon and Neptune City Police Departments. In 1988, Steve graduated from the police academy and began a near thirty-year career as a law enforcement officer. He was a dedicated public servant who worked his way up the ranks of the Bradley Beach Police Department and eventually became a captain. When his wife retired from her career at the end of 2015, Steve went along with her and retired from law enforcement before the end of the year.

As a family, Steve and Natalie—as well as their son Stephen—share a love of cooking. Even before Steve and Natalie retired from their respective careers, they spent many weekends catering parties for friends and family. In fact, shortly before their retirement, they formed Creative Catering by Natalie LLC.

Natalie was the mastermind behind the recipes and menu, which mostly featured traditional catering options. In particular, they offered American

and Italian cuisine and a variety of desserts. As Natalie brought her vision to reality, her husband and son provided manual labor and moral support.

Like his parents, Stephen never thought he'd become one of the state's top food truckers. Out of high school, he attended Ocean County College, where he earned a degree in computer science. He originally intended to transition to a four-year school but instead decided to use what he had learned (web design and development) to help build and manage the websites and social media pages for the family business. Within two years, he had become a partner in the business and took over event booking and planning. When the family founded the Shore Good Eats 'N' Treats food truck in 2016, he managed that as well.

TAKING THEIR IDEA TO-GO

The new food truck allowed the Fahnholz family to take many of their catering menu items and desserts on the road. But Shore Good doesn't just focus on a couple of themed items for their menu; they put their inventiveness on full display. Like the truck's wrap, each one of Shore Goods' menu items is eye catching and (unlike the wrap) mouthwatering. Though the truck serves a variety of comfort food, it specializes in fried gourmet egg rolls.

Before the Fahnholzes bought their first truck, they would regularly attend festivals, serving from tented booths. During one Irish festival, Natalie wanted to set her food apart and decided to make Reuben egg rolls. The item sold so well that she ran out of the filling and was left with only several bundles of egg roll wrappers. The family improvised and started rolling their cheesesteak in the wrappers and deep frying them. Those, too, quickly sold out, giving the Fahnholz family an idea for a whole assortment of new menu items.

Shore Good offers more than forty different fillings and continually builds on their selection. Fan favorites include buffalo chicken, cheesesteak, mac and cheese, pulled pork and Southwest chicken. Shore Good also puts those flavors into compact sandwiches and wraps and offers tacos, sliders and more for catered events.

GROWING THE BUSINESS

In January 2018, the Fahnholz family decided to bring their menu to a brick-and-mortar. They opened their own café of the same name in Neptune City. The café is open for breakfast and lunch, with a similar menu to the truck, in addition to some other selections exclusive to the storefront.

The Shore Good Eats 'N' Treats café gives guests their pick of platters, sandwiches, waffles, omelettes and wraps. Likewise, lunch is an equally opulent affair with different sandwiches, wraps, egg rolls, homemade soups, salads, grilled cheeses, burgers and wings to choose from. As for dessert, patrons can select from a range of cakes, cupcakes, muffins, cookies, brownies, cannoli, scones, pies and assorted pastries. They also offer fudge brownies, apple pie and an assortment of cheesecake flavors, all in egg roll form.

For several years, Steve, Natalie and Stephen were the complete team behind Creative Catering by Natalie and Shore Good Eats 'N' Treats. They used their education and professional experience from three separate fields to build a successful enterprise. The Fahnholz family has a true passion for the culinary field, and their unwavering support for one another has made them a force to be reckoned with—something they are passing on to their next wave of crew members as the Shore Good team continues to grow.

Q&A with Co-Founder Steve Fahnholz

What was your first year in business like?

We got our first truck in May 2016. We came up with Shore Good Eats 'N' Treats so we could offer many of our catering menu options as well as our fresh-made desserts. We didn't want to be known as a one-dimensional truck. We were very worried that because we were new and no one knew us that we wouldn't be able to get into events and the other food truck owners would just look at us as competition and wouldn't be friendly. But once we got out there, we realized it was just the opposite. All the other food truck owners were so friendly and helpful. They helped us fine-tune our operation and helped us to get into events, and before long, we were standing on our own two feet. The food truck industry truly is one big family, and we all help each other.

How has your food truck evolved over the past few years?

We started out doing public events, and then we started getting requests to bring our truck to private events like birthday parties and graduations. Soon thereafter, we started getting calls to do corporate events, and it has been building by leaps and bounds since. We had so many people asking where they could get our food all the time, so we decided to open a café in January 2018 and feature our own signature breakfast and lunch items, as well as menu options from the truck. There was such a demand for our truck that we added a second truck in January 2020.

Does your truck's menu change depending on the event/venue or time of year?

Yes, we do festival/event–specific menus in order to best serve our customers. We have special menu options that are only available certain times of the year. For instance, our Pumpkin Cheesecake Egg Roll can only be found at festivals in the fall.

Tell us about your desserts. Are they usually available on your truck?

Natalie's true passion is baking. She scratch makes desserts every day and fills our bakery case and the truck with the most incredible desserts, from cookies, brownies, scones, cinnamon buns—you name it. By far, her favorite dessert to make for people are her assorted cupcakes. Try one and you'll be hooked for sure.

What are some popular items on your truck?

We have a few, but definitely our gourmet and dessert egg rolls and our butterfly fries with assorted toppings. We serve our butterfly fries plain or with different toppings such as Jalapeño Hog or Cheesy Bacon Ranch. We have won several awards for both the egg rolls and butterfly fries.

How would you describe the Shore Good Eats 'N' Treats storefront?

Our café is a comfortable beach-themed atmosphere serving large platters and overstuffed sandwiches for breakfast and lunch. It is not your average burger and sandwich place. We put a "Shore Good Twist" on everything we do, like serving our Thanksgiving sandwich on a waffle made from our house-made stuffing. We scratch make most menu items, like our short rib, pulled pork, corned beef, turkey, mac and cheese, etc.

What is one thing you wish you knew before you started your food truck?

I wish someone would have told me I would be working harder than I ever have my entire life. Unless you are in the business, I really don't think people understand how hard food truck owners work just to make sure the quality and consistency of our products are always exceptional in order to keep customers happy. But I have to admit that seeing the smiles on their faces is very fulfilling.

CHAPTER 15

KIERSTEN'S CREATIONS

Key Lime Pops

Key Lime Curd
4.55 grams powdered gelatin
585 grams sugar
585 grams eggs
336 grams key lime juice
390 grams butter
Lime zest (optional)
1 drop green food coloring (optional)

Graham Crumble
240 grams graham cracker crumbs
182 grams butter, melted
100 grams granulated sugar
2 grams salt

For Pops
Popsicle sticks
Popsicle mold (or ice cube tray, small paper/plastic cups)

Key Lime Curd: Bloom gelatin in cold water.

Combine sugar and eggs in a bowl and mix well.

Bring key lime juice to a boil on medium-high heat. Temper boiling key lime juice into the eggs and sugar.

Bring juice, sugar and eggs to a boil. Boil for 1 minute, stirring continuously. Remove from heat and add bloomed gelatin, butter, lime zest and food coloring. Refrigerate until needed.

Note: If you overcook the curd, your eggs will become scrambled. If it is slightly overcooked, you can use an immersion blender or standard blender to smooth it out and then strain it. The texture may not be perfectly consistent, but it will still work.

Graham Crumble: Combine graham cracker crumbs, melted butter, sugar and salt. Mix well. Bake on a sheet pan at 350 degrees Fahrenheit until just golden brown.

Remove from oven, allow to cool and then put in a food processor. Store in an airtight container until needed.

Key Lime Pops: Once ready to prepare the Key Lime Pops, remove the Key lime curd from the fridge.

In popsicle mold, alternate adding layers of first curd, then crumbles, beginning with curd and ending with crumbles. Insert sticks and place mold in freezer. Freeze overnight or as long as desired.

When ready to enjoy, just pop them right out of your mold. Leftovers can be stored in an airtight bag in the freezer.

~~~

Peanut Butter Pie

Oreo Crust
350 grams Oreo crumble
125 grams butter, melted
2 pie tins

Peanut Butter Filling
250 grams heavy cream
500 grams peanut butter
750 grams cream cheese
250 grams powdered sugar

Whipped Cream
500 grams heavy cream
200 grams powdered sugar

Ganache
200 grams heavy cream
200 grams dark chocolate

Oreo Crust: Combine Oreo crumble and melted butter. Use half to layer each pie tin.

Peanut Butter Filling: Whip heavy cream to stiff peaks, then put aside.

Combine peanut butter, cream cheese and powdered sugar in a bowl and beat until smooth.

Fold together the whipped cream and peanut butter mixture. Store in refrigerator until needed.

Whipped Cream: Combine heavy cream with powdered sugar in a bowl and whip until stiff peaks. Store in refrigerator until needed.

Ganache: Boil heavy cream. Place dark chocolate in a medium bowl, then pour boiling heavy cream over dark chocolate and let sit for 1 minute before stirring together. Store at room temperature until needed.

Peanut Butter Pie: Scoop half of peanut butter filling on top of Oreo crust, lining each pie tin. Spread until even.

Top peanut butter filling layer with fresh whipped cream and spread evenly.

Pour ganache on top of whipped cream layer and spread to entirely cover the whipped cream. (You can use a knife or spatula to help cover the outside of the pie with ganache.)

Put a scoop of peanut butter in a pastry bag (or plastic resealable bag with a small tip cut off the corner). Drizzle peanut butter on top of the pie.

Optional: Add toppings, such as chocolate chips, peanut butter cups and Oreo pieces. Store in fridge until ready to eat or serve.

~~~

Born to Bake

Kiersten Connor wanted her own food truck from the time she was twelve. She remembers one afternoon back in middle school driving in the car with her parents and seeing a box truck for sale on the side of the road. Had she been old enough—and had the sufficient funds—to purchase it, she knew exactly what she'd turn it into.

"We should open up a dessert truck one day," Kiersten told her mom. Her mother liked the idea, but knowing how fleeting children's dreams can be, she didn't give it much stock. But for Kiersten, her dream never wavered.

That same year, she took a job reffing youth soccer games in order to start saving for her very own truck. She was infatuated with the idea of running a business, especially a gourmet food truck, which at the time was unheard of in New Jersey. She always had a sweet tooth growing up, craving everything from cake to candy. This was paired with a love for baking. In fact, she perfected many of her recipes before she even got her driver's license. Kiersten enjoyed making cookies and brownies from scratch, often putting her own twist on modern treats. After watching TLC's *Cake Boss*, she was inspired to get creative with her cakes.

Laser Focused

Over the following decade, nothing knocked Kiersten off her path. While in high school, Kiersten planned to attend culinary school to learn about cooking, baking and the industry. So right after graduation, she enrolled at the Culinary Institute of America in Hyde Park, New York. She earned her associate's degree in baking and pastry and then stayed for two more years to earn a bachelor's in food business management.

After graduating from culinary school, Kiersten prepared for her enterprise. She continued working to earn more money and used her savings to buy a short bus off Craigslist. But the truck had its problems. The vehicle was not up to code, and her business would have to wait. It took a few months—and a lot of help from her father and uncle—to renovate the truck.

All the while, Kiersten worked on her menu. She devised a collection of sweet treats, creating a variety of desserts on a modest menu with some rotating items. Of course, there are popular options like chocolate chip, peanut butter and Funfetti cookies. Then there are signature items, like the option to select two cookies and sandwich them with a scoop of ice cream. There's also a selection of cheesecakes, including traditional, strawberry shortcake and even brownie.

Kiersten also offers frozen treats on the truck, including ice cream and sundaes, as well as strawberry lemonade and key lime pie frozen popsicles. She even offers cold brew floats complete with coffee, vanilla ice cream, chocolate syrup, caramel sauce and whipped cream.

STILL DREAMIN'

The Kiersten's Creations food truck launched in early 2021, boasting a bright pink exterior adorned with sprinkled windows and a glowing logo. Unlike most trucks that cook right in the vehicle, Kiersten does much of her baking and prep work at her commissary kitchen prior to an event. She and her team bake from scratch, and every item is fresh. As a self-proclaimed "junk food junkie," she knows fellow sweet tooths can taste the difference.

Kiersten has been working in the food business for a decade now. She never takes for granted the fact that her childhood dream came true. She's always developing new recipes and "creations," bringing something new to each event. She's also mindful of how lucky she is to be fulfilling the plan she shared with her mom all those years ago.

Q&A with Owner Kiersten Connor

Going back to when you were a kid, what made you want to specialize in dessert?

I have a big sweet tooth. There is no other way to say it [laughs]. I was like the junk food junkie. You know, Halloween: loved it. Only went for the candy. Never enjoy dressing up—just wanted the candy. And Carlo's Bakery, when *Cake Boss* started, that heightened my interest.

What was your first full season like with Kiersten's Creations?

It was way more than I imagined—more hours and, honestly, way more fun. I met the most amazing people. Everybody is so awesome and supportive of each other. We really are like a family, and it's the most fun and most rewarding job I've ever had.

I quote somebody that I work with, who always says, "We're in the smile industry." And we really are [laughs]. We're always out there just to make people happy, and that makes us happy in return.

What different types of items do you offer?

We offer a cheesecake, chocolate mousse, baked goods and we do ice cream sandwiches and sundaes. And then we always throw in some fun items; I like to keep things fresh and get my creative side going. We like to incorporate seasonal as well as event-specific items.

What are some of your most popular items?

Our most popular cheesecake would be the strawberry shortcake cheesecake. And then we have a peanut butter chocolate mousse that people really love. Our ice cream sandwiches are my favorite. You can mix and match between any of our baked goods with vanilla ice cream in between. You can get even a brownie and a Funfetti cookie with ice cream in between. The cookies are always fresh and soft, so you can always try something a little different.

What kind of catering options do you offer?

We can do with or without the bus. You can order right through email—or any way you'd like to get in contact: phone call, text, Instagram. We do corporate events, weddings, post-weddings, birthday parties, holiday menus, really any private party you're looking for. We can come with the truck, too.

Our orders are strictly dessert, but they're not restricted to my usual items. So, for example, if a customer came to me and said, "I just love s'mores," we could come up with a special dessert for you, whether we make a nice s'mores topping on a mousse or its own special item.

PART IV

· ·

SOUTH JERSEY FOOD TRUCKS

· ·

CHAPTER 16

DAN'S WAFFLES

BBQ Pulled Pork Waffle

While Dan's personal waffle recipe is a closely guarded secret, he was happy to provide a slightly modified recipe for readers to try at home.

Liege Waffles (Makes 15 waffles)

1 ½ tablespoons light brown sugar
1 ¾ teaspoons active dry yeast
⅓ cup lukewarm water
2 cups all-purpose flour
½ teaspoon salt
3 large eggs
1 teaspoon pure vanilla extract
2 sticks unsalted butter (about 1 cup, plus more for brushing)
1 cup Belgian pearl sugar*

Dan's BBQ Pulled Pork (Makes 12 servings)

Requires: *Slow cooker or pressure cooker*
3 pounds boneless pork shoulder/butt or pork sirloin roast
1 teaspoon coarse kosher salt
½ teaspoon coarsely ground black pepper
2 cups water or low-sodium chicken broth
2 tablespoons liquid smoke
3 cups barbecue sauce (plus more for serving)

BBQ Pulled Pork Waffles
Belgian Liege Waffle
Dan's BBQ Pulled Pork
Barbecue sauce
Coleslaw
Pickles

Liege Waffles: In a small bowl, whisk the brown sugar and yeast into the lukewarm water and let stand until foamy, about 5 minutes.

In the bowl of a standing mixer fitted with paddle attachment, mix the flour with salt. Make a well in the center of the bowl and pour in the yeast mixture. Mix at medium speed until shaggy, about 1 minute. Add the eggs one at a time, mixing for 20 seconds between each.

Whisk vanilla extract with 1 cup of melted butter. With the mixer at medium-low, gradually add butter mixture until smooth. The batter will be thick and very sticky.

Cover the bowl with plastic wrap and let the batter rise in a warm place until doubled in size, about 1 hour and 45 minutes.

Stir the pearl sugar into the risen batter. Cover again and let rest for 15 minutes.

Preheat a Belgian waffle iron and brush with melted butter.

Gently stir the batter to deflate. Using about 2 tablespoons of batter for each, cook until golden and crisp.

Brush the waffle iron with melted butter as needed.

Transfer the waffles to plates or keep them warm in a 225-degree Fahrenheit oven until ready to serve.

*The key ingredient for these waffles. Adds pops of sweetness and caramelizes to make the exterior crisp.

Dan's BBQ Pulled Pork: Cut the pork roast into 4-inch pieces. (This step is optional, but it helps to cook the pork a bit faster and more evenly.)

Season the pork on all sides with salt and pepper.

Add water or broth and liquid smoke to slow cooker or pressure cooker. Then add pork.

Cover and cook on low for 8 to 10 hours, or on high for 5 to 6 hours, until the pork is fall-apart tender.

Remove the pork from the slow/pressure cooker and discard most of the remaining liquid. Leave about ¼ cup or so of the juices.

Shred the pork using a couple forks. It should easily fall apart into pieces.

Place the meat back into the slow/pressure cooker and add barbecue sauce. You can either heat through or keep your slow cooker on warm for several hours, until ready to serve.

BBQ Pulled Pork Waffle: Prepare Belgian Liege Waffle and Dan's BBQ Pulled Pork. Then pile pulled pork atop waffle.

Pour additional barbecue sauce over pulled pork.

Serve with coleslaw and pickles on the side.

Notes:

Adding time: If you get to the end of cooking time for either the slow cooker or pressure cooker and the pork is not tender enough, simply add more time until it is fall-apart tender.

Alternate meat: Bone-in pork roasts can also be used with this recipe. Cooking time should be about the same. Discard bone before shredding.

Dan's Famous Chicken and Waffles

Dan's Sausage Gravy

1 pound ground pork sausage
2 tablespoons butter
⅓ cup flour
3 cups milk
¼ teaspoon garlic powder
¼ teaspoon seasoned salt
¼ teaspoon salt, plus more to taste
1 teaspoon black pepper, plus more to taste

Chicken and Waffles

Belgian Liege Waffle
Fried chicken
Dan's Sausage Gravy
Shredded cheddar, sharp or mild
Maple syrup
Hot sauce

Dan's Sausage Gravy: Brown the sausage in a large skillet over medium-high heat until no longer pink.

Add butter to the pan and stir it around until melted.

Sprinkle flour over the sausage and stir for 2 minutes.

Pour the milk into the sausage and flour mixture slowly, whisking constantly until smooth.

Whisk in garlic powder, seasoned salt, salt and black pepper.

Taste the gravy and adjust seasoning if necessary.

Dan's Famous Chicken and Waffles: Prepare Belgian Liege Waffle and top with your favorite fried chicken recipe.

Prepare Dan's Sausage Gravy and pour over chicken and waffle.

Sprinkle shredded cheddar atop chicken and waffles.

Serve with warm maple syrup and hot sauce on the side.

No Time for Waffling

Chef Daniel Hover hails from the Buckeye State. He was raised and went to school in Ohio, where he first developed an interest in cuisine. Cooking and experimenting with food intrigued him, so when he turned sixteen, he began working in kitchens in his home state. After graduating from high school—rather than immediately enrolling in secondary education—he continued to work his way up.

By his early twenties, Daniel craved something more. He enjoyed his line of work but wanted to grow and expand his culinary discipline. He enrolled at the Culinary Institute of America and relocated to New York, juggling his education with jobs at various Manhattan eateries. Upon graduating, he again dove straight into the restaurant industry.

His career then transitioned from New York City to the Garden State, where he thrived. In addition to running the kitchen of a South Jersey country club, he became co-owner of a seafood restaurant in Voorhees Township, Camden County. The restaurant chugged along for eighteen years before Daniel needed some type of change. So he and his partners closed the restaurant while Daniel took some time off with his wife, Russel. But he didn't stay idle for long.

A New Venture

Just days into his "break," Daniel and Russel were brainstorming business ideas. It wasn't long before Russel suggested purchasing a food truck. In 2015, the couple bought a used truck in desperate need of some TLC. They spent two years building it out, upgrading the equipment, wrapping the exterior and making the vehicle safe for themselves on the road. By 2017, they were ready to go live with a completely unique theme: bubble waffles.

During those two years working on the truck, the couple spent a lot of their free time discussing what they wanted to sell. First, they considered different American staples. Likewise, Russel—who was born in the Philippines—suggested distinct Filipino dishes. The two explored Asian cuisine and discovered they could easily prepare and make bubble waffles for their food truck. No one in the area was doing anything like it, and the versatility of waffles meant they could offer lunch, dinner and dessert items.

However, by their second year, Daniel and Russel decided to adjust their theme. They liked the idea of waffles, but the cost of the necessary equipment to make bubble waffles specifically was not sustainable. So they pivoted to a menu of Belgian Liege waffles, the specialty of Dan's Waffles to this day.

Now Anytime Is Waffle Time

The Dan's Waffles food truck serves all sorts of waffle combos. Their most popular meal is chicken and waffles. In fact, it's not uncommon for the truck to sell out of chicken before an event is over. Another fan favorite is the barbecue pulled pork piled atop a warm waffle. Keeping with the theme, patrons can also purchase waffle fries—loaded or simply salted—as well as a waffle cone filled with either mac and cheese or fried chicken and buffalo sauce.

As for dessert options, they range from a simple scoop of vanilla between two fresh Belgian waffles to their signature dessert waffles. These include Oreo S'mores, Salted Caramel Apple, Bananas Foster and, specifically for adults, the Strawberry Margarita: a Belgian waffle topped with strawberries, tequila and lime. Dan's Waffles also offers loaded gourmet shakes and their unique Dan's Donut (a warm cinnamon sugar doughnut filled with vanilla ice cream). For special events, customers can order Chef Dan's Famous Triple Coconut Cream Pie, which was featured on the Food Network's *The Best Thing I Ever Ate*.

Daniel has had a fulfilling career in the culinary industry. He loves his truck, which he created with his wife and also pays homage to his mother's culture and ancestry. Despite the success of Dan's Waffles, Daniel and Russel continue to strive for greater heights, expanding their menu and challenging themselves in new ways. Today, they're working side by side making waffles. Tomorrow, their next endeavor could be another of New Jersey's premier food trucks.

Q&A with Owner Daniel Hover

What was the first day for Dan's Waffles like?

I still remember the very first day; it was the centennial of Pennsauken, and it was crazy. We had the longest line; people actually came back even after the event was closed. They went home and came back to get more food [laughs]. It was really something.

Where did the waffle idea come from?

I visited a small place up in Manhattan that was doing the Asian bubble waffles. And so that's actually what we started doing in the very beginning.

Our main thing was bubble waffles. Then I asked some people around and talked to some people in the industry, and they said don't really do one thing; have maybe a couple of options for people that might be unsure, because really, at that time, bubble waffles weren't even known around here.

Based on bubble waffles, there's one person in Manhattan, a couple of people out in LA. That's it [laughs]. And they're all brick-and-mortars. Nobody's doing it on a truck.

What are bubble waffles?

They're an octagonal-shaped waffle, special waffle iron and press. And there are almost egg-like shape indentations in the waffle iron. And the batter is really, really rich. A lot of eggs, almost like cake. It's the number-one street food in Hong Kong. But the people are making them on cast-iron grills over a charcoal fire. That's how they make them, and they just put them in a paper bag and serve them.

But the waffle irons that I had to come over from China. They're terribly expensive and were taking three to four months to get at that time, and they don't last. I mean, I don't know if it's the 110 voltage versus the 220. But I've had some last two hours. I've had some last two months, but I've never had any last over two months. Maybe in a different environment, maybe if you're in a small café or at home or something like that; maybe it's OK where you're only making a few. But going into these events, I was making two, three, four hundred bubble waffles, just going crazy with it. And the machines, I think, were just overworked. Also being on for eight hours in a day, maybe the heating elements just couldn't handle that. I still have a couple for small events, small parties, but they're not used much anymore. As they say, you never forget your roots [laughs], and that's how it started.

What other types of menu items do you offer?

Right now, it's very broad. I mean, more broad than most food trucks. I try to stick with the waffle theme, because, of course, our Belgian waffles are front and center. That's our main item. It's kind of like an homage to my mother; she was a Danish pastry chef. And in fact, that's the only difference between the traditional Belgian waffle recipe. I don't use the Belgian pearl sugar; I use her Danish sugar. A little bit smaller, but it doesn't melt under high heat. So rather than mixing the sugar into the waffle, which would be a traditional Belgian waffle, we go and dip the raw dough into the sugar, and then they bake on the outside. That's why it looks very unique. When it comes out, you get a little crunch from those sugar crystals. It's really delicious.

What would you say are the most popular items on your menu?

Definitely chicken and waffles. That is probably the number-one thing. And also some of our sweet waffles. We get a lot of requests for the Oreo S'mores waffle and Bananas Foster waffle. I did barbecue pulled pork on the waffle, and that's become very popular; it really turned into something surprising. We just put some coleslaw on the side and some pickles. The sweet, sour, salty and the smokiness of it goes perfect with the Belgian waffle.

But then we do waffle cones with chicken inside with multiple sauces. We do waffle bowls. We put mac and cheese in that, topped with chicken, barbecue pulled pork or bacon. I also do waffle fries; just kind of stick with the theme. That's all on the savory side. Then I also do some gourmet milkshakes, and that's always a killer for the kids because of that unicorn milkshake. It has a candy twist in it, Fruity Pebbles on it. We rim the glass with chocolate fudge and sprinkles, put a little bit of a strawberry syrup around the sides, put vanilla milkshake on the inside, and then we even top it off with colored marshmallows and Pocky sticks and even an edible butterfly [laughs]. We have a picture of it up on our truck, and every single time a little kid walks by it, they're hooked.

Do you offer any catering options?

Yes, we do. We customize everything according to a customer's needs, because we do parties for fifty guests and up. Our biggest one so far has been about eight hundred people. And again, everything is solely custom based on a person's needs and budget.

And there are so many factors too, because I have such a varied menu. Do you want dessert, an entrée or both? We try to offer the best, whether it's a wedding, bar mitzvah or corporate event. We've just about done it all.

CHAPTER 17

GOOD FOOD = GOOD MOOD

Applewood Bacon and Gorgonzola Stuff'd Burger

Required

Griddle (cast-iron skillet or heavy sauté pan will also work)
Canola oil, for griddle
Heat-resistant lid or cover for sauté pan
Spatula

(Yield: 2 burgers)

16 ounces ground beef (preferably Angus)
4 slices thick-cut applewood-smoked bacon, cooked crisp, cut in half
(4 half slices total)
6 ounces crumbled gorgonzola cheese
Salt and ground black pepper, to taste
2 brioche buns, halved and toasted
2 green leaf lettuce leaves, cleaned
2 ripe tomato slices

Break apart ground beef into four equal balls and form into equal patties. Two of these will be your tops, and the other two will be your bottoms. Lay two cooked bacon half-strips on two of the bottom patties, staying away from the outer edges.

Separate gorgonzola cheese into equal parts and form in palm of hand into two balls and then into flat mini cheese patties. Lay each cheese patty flat onto the half bacon slices on the bottom beef patties.

To complete the burger stuffing, place the last bacon halves on top of the gorgonzola cheese. Now place burger tops onto each filled bottom patty. Press down on the center and edges. Pick up the whole stuffed burger in the palm of your hand and work the edges together to form one solid burger.

Season both sides with salt and pepper.

Heat a cast-iron skillet or heavy sauté pan to medium-high heat and add a touch of canola oil. Add both burgers to the pan. Be careful—there will be splatters. Cook uncovered for about 2 minutes to create a nice sear on the meat. Cover with lid and continue to cook 2 to 3 minutes.

Uncover and press the patty down gently to spread patty back out without squeezing out the melting cheese filling. Carefully flip burger patty, cover and finish cooking for about 3 minutes.

Take a peek to make sure the filling is completely melted by poking a thin fork into the burger.

Remove from pan and let rest 1 to 2 minutes, as filling will be hot.

Build Stuff'd Burger on toasted brioche buns and top with lettuce and tomato.

Enjoy!

~~~

The Cure for Hanger

The term *hangry* is used to describe someone who is irritable as a result of hunger. So it stands to reason that if hunger can lead to a bad mood, surely a satisfying meal can lead to a good mood. This is exactly the idea behind Good Food = Good Mood, a food truck owned by Dean and Emily Hodecker that specializes in burgers.

The truck began its journey in April 2016 offering twists on traditional burgers and fries. In particular, the Good Mood truck started off specializing in stuffed burgers: burger patties encircling a selection of cheeses such as gorgonzola or roasted jalapeño cheddar. From there, the husband-and-wife duo experimented with finding the perfect side dishes, including their crispy, all-natural French fries.

Dean and Emily's relationship predates not only their food truck but also their professional culinary careers. The two have been working in restaurants since their teenage years but didn't begin dating until they both progressed through the ranks of kitchens throughout the state and surrounding areas. After individually experiencing managing their own large operations, their aspirations turned toward owning their own business.

Dean and Emily chose to start a food truck—as opposed to a brick-and-mortar—due to its lower start-up cost. Serving food in a mobile rig also allows the duo to take their food to wider audiences, which is why Good Mood frequently travels throughout the Garden State and surrounding areas most of the year.

From Stuffings to Toppings

Throughout Good Mood's six years in business, the menu has undergone only minor changes. The most obvious alteration is the removal of their once signature stuffed burgers. Of course, they still offer their traditional burger, but now they have a number of specialty burgers with assorted toppings. This includes the Mac Burger, a bacon cheeseburger topped with Good Mood's fried mac and cheese; the Truffle Burger, topped with melted

Left to right: Avocado BLT Burger, Mac Burger and Avocado Fries.

Parmesan and truffle aioli; the BBQ Pulled Pork Cheeseburger, covered in pulled pork, cilantro slaw, chipotle aioli and scallions; and the Avocado BLT Cheeseburger, capped with bacon, fried avocado and chipotle aioli.

Likewise, they offer loaded fries with a variety of toppings. Menu options range from Pulled Pork Fries and Buffalo Fries to Honey Mustard Bacon Fries and Truffle Fries. Additional sides on the Good Mood menu include Dean and Emily's homemade Parmesan Rice Balls. The truck even has a few Latin surprises in the form of pulled pork and avocado tacos.

JUST THE TWO OF US

Dean and Emily are the complete unit behind Good Food = Good Mood. The menu, the recipes, the truck, the booking, the social media, the paperwork—they handle it all. Through the ups and downs, the mundane tasks and the exciting events, the couple is on the road throughout the week and every single weekend. After spending most of their lives side by side, it's no surprise they remain an inseparable duo to this day. The successful food truck is more than proof of Dean and Emily's culinary capabilities and business savvy; it's also a testament to their steadfast relationship and how a couple's unabated diligence, determination and teamwork can help them to achieve their dreams.

Q&A with Co-Owners Dean Hodecker and Emily Hodecker

Did you two meet somewhere along your culinary journey?

Dean: No, we've actually known each other for fifteen years now. We met in elementary school through friends of our friends. We were friends for a while and then finally got serious after high school. We both started working a lot of kitchen jobs and decided that culinary school was going to be the way to go. So we decided to go together, as a package deal, to the Culinary Institute. We told them we wanted to go through this together. We actually were in the same class. We did all our classes side by side. It was pretty cool.

How does your culinary experience translate to the food truck business?

Dean: Well, when we started out, we began as line cooks in restaurants. So, you know, it's pretty much what we're doing on a daily basis on the food truck; we're cooking to order as quickly as we can with the best ingredients possible.

When we were hired to work in the food service industry, it was all the office obligations. We did the hiring, the firing, the payroll, the paperwork financial statements. So we got our experience in the kitchen straight out of culinary school and then grew into management-type positions.

One of the most impressive elements of Good Food = Good Mood is the truck itself. Tell us about it.

Dean: The first thing we planned when we decided to open the business was our menu. This way, we were able to base the specifications of the truck on our menu. So everything is as smooth as possible. So whoever's working the grill, all your ingredients are right below you; whoever's working the finishing station doing all the garnishes, the fryer and everything is right around you. So nobody has to move from their station. The whole idea was to make it as efficient as possible.

I pretty much took old-school graph paper, drew out exactly where I wanted this equipment, what equipment I wanted to put where and I brought it to our builder, who then made real layouts and worked on getting the right equipment and doing the final build of the truck itself. It was a whole process. A lot of wheels were turning for about a year before we decided that we were happy with the way it is.

What's the most important lesson you've learned since starting the truck?

Dean: I think one of the most important things we've learned is networking with other trucks. It's important developing relationships with other trucks, because at the end of the day, one hand washes the other. You help each other out and basically turn into families at events. We're all going through the same struggles, and we're all going through the same processes with the permits and all the procedures that we have to follow.

Besides the Mac Burger, what are your most popular items?

Dean: Behind the Mac Burger is the Avocado BLT Cheeseburger. Our most popular loaded fries are the Truffle Fries, which are crispy fries topped with a black truffle aioli sauce, Parmesan cheese and some sliced black truffles over the top of it. Then there's our BBQ Pulled Pork Fries, with slow-roasted pulled pork, topped with cilantro coleslaw, chipotle aioli and fresh scallions. That's also very dramatic looking. It gets people excited.

Emily: Our most popular side is the Avocado Fries. They're fresh avocado sliced, breaded, seasoned and fried. It's topped with two sauces—the jalapeño cilantro aioli and the chipotle aioli—and then it's topped off with some scallions.

What types of catering packages does Good Food = Good Mood offer?

Dean: Everything from the basic burgers and fries all the way up to our full-blown menu with plenty of choices. It all depends on how big the party is, what their price point is and what exactly their needs are. And we also allow add-on items if a package is missing a food item you'd like.

We've done parties from twenty-five people all the way up to seven hundred people. So we know what we're doing when it comes to catering [laughs].

CHAPTER 18

THE GRATEFUL GOURMET

Cosmic Candied Sriracha Bacon

Required
Oven-safe baking rack
Nonstick cooking spray
Baking sheet

1 package thick-sliced hickory-smoked bacon
½ cup Sriracha sauce
½ cup brown sugar
2 tablespoons pepper

Preheat oven to 350 degrees Fahrenheit.
Spray baking rack with nonstick spray.

Place bacon on rack. Brush bacon with ¼ cup of sriracha sauce, then sprinkle with ¼ cup of brown sugar. Sprinkle bacon with 1 tablespoon of pepper.

Bake for 15 to 20 minutes, until nearly crisp.

Take bacon out, repeat process with remainder of ingredients and bake for another 5 minutes (or until desired crispness).

Take bacon out of the oven and cool for a couple minutes before serving.

Friend of the Deviled Egg

Deviled Eggs
6 large eggs
Cold water
1 teaspoon Dijon mustard
3 dashes Louisiana hot sauce
Salt, to taste
¼ teaspoon freshly ground black pepper
1 tablespoon dill pickle relish
3 tablespoons mayonnaise
Paprika, for garnish

Candied Bacon (for garnish)
Vegetable oil
8 slices thick-cut bacon, diced
½ cup brown sugar

Deviled Eggs: Rinse eggs with warm water and place in a small saucepan. Cover completely with cold water. Place the pan over medium-high heat and bring to a boil.

Turn off heat, cover saucepan and let sit for 10 to 12 minutes.

Drain, rinse under cold water and peel.

Let cool in the refrigerator, loosely covered, for 15 minutes.

Candied Bacon: While eggs are in the fridge, heat a thin layer of vegetable oil in saucepan on medium-high heat for 5 minutes.

Fry chopped bacon in pan.

Drain bacon on paper towels, saving 1 to 2 tablespoons of bacon grease.

Put brown sugar into pan and begin to melt with bacon grease, stirring in bacon. Once bacon and sugar get to the candy stage, remove from heat and put on a plate.

Combine: After 15 minutes in the fridge, halve eggs lengthwise and carefully scoop out yolks. Place yolks in a bowl and mash with a fork.

Add mustard, hot sauce, salt, pepper and relish. Then stir in mayonnaise.

Fill each egg white with yolk mixture with a piping bag. Top with candied bacon and then paprika.

~~~

Grateful for Grandma's Cooking

Desiree Bagnell was raised on a seventy-acre farm in the rural hills of northern central Pennsylvania. She was one of six kids terrorizing their stay-at-home mom—but all the while, Mom enthralled them with her favorite interest: cooking.

Desiree's mother cooked every meal. The family grew all of their vegetables, and her parents wasted nothing. While her father traveled for business, her mom stayed home, tended to the crops, prepared meals and taught her children how to cook.

The family didn't consume much meat. Most of what they cooked was plant based—*years* before it was popular. Using only ingredients from the garden, none of what Desiree and her siblings ate was processed. She still laughs when she thinks about the "snacks" she and her siblings used to enjoy as kids, atypical from the goodies many of us grew up gobbling down. "I grew up with an industrial-sized refrigerator in my house when I was a kid," said Desiree, "so we would have like a bushel of apples in there, and we'd eat salad for snacks."

Desiree's grandmother was also a great cook, and the two maternal generations made sure to pass down all of their tips and tricks of the kitchen.

Ever since Desiree was big enough to stand on a stool and stir, she was helping her family in the kitchen, assisting with a variety of dishes. Her family was adept at making plant-based meals mixed with delicious sauces and dressings. The continuous stream of homemade meals was always healthy and tasty.

Gratitude Goes a Long Way

Even years after moving away from her childhood farm, Desiree never lost the bug for cooking. In fact, it turned into a full-blown passion. While she went to school and started a career in recruitment and human resources, she managed her own kitchen at home. She was the chef of the Bagnell household, elated to share her recipes with her own children, much like her mother and grandmother. However, Desiree desired to share her cooking with an even larger audience. Along with her family and friends, visitors who got a taste for Desiree's cooking had nothing but glowing feedback. The responses gave her the push she needed to start her own culinary business.

Throughout the early 2000s, Desiree spent nearly all of her free time developing a concept. She soon started her own catering company, My Retro Bistro. She continued to work her full-time administrative career, taking catering on as a part-time venture. She started off working birthday parties, anniversary celebrations and baby showers—events that were small and manageable. But she was working nearly sixty hours a week for her full-time job, leaving her with barely enough time to prep and work smaller gatherings. Once My Retro Bistro started to take off, all of a sudden she was catering larger events like weddings.

For nearly two decades, Desiree balanced a full-time career, a side catering business and family life. She enjoyed the challenges and the rewards her culinary endeavor provided, so much so that she wanted to make it a larger part of her life. So at the end of 2019, Desiree and her husband, Paul, bought an old 1957 Canned Ham camper from a North Carolina fisherman. The trailer was worn, used and needed work. Once the trailer was built out and customized, Desiree was ready for her next hat: food trucking.

Leading up to the truck's launch, Desiree offered contactless delivery. Each week, she posted a menu on social media; customers would order what they wanted and then set up a time and date for delivery. She enjoyed getting creative with her menus and, more so, being able to feed other families. She continued this service until her truck was ready for the road.

READY TO ROCK

In the fall of 2020, the Grateful Gourmet was born. Desiree describes her cuisine as southern-inspired comfort food, blending influences from her cooking and regional experiences. She likes to whip up traditional dishes, like her Hell in a Bucket Hot Chicken Sandwich, while also getting creative with items like her Friend of the Deviled Eggs. Similarly, she offers a Celestial Mac and Cheese with seven different types of cheeses. There's also a tender pork sandwich with apple butter. For those who like to eat a little healthier, there's the Franklin's Brussels, paired with her secret sauce. Desiree has no shortage of ideas, and every season she expands her menu. When the off-season comes around, she goes back to her delivery service and also offers some other exclusive specials.

With her truck, Desiree is able to do what she loves every single day. Moreover, the Grateful Gourmet enables Desiree to share a bit of her upbringing with fellow New Jerseyans. Each item on her menu is adeptly named, thoughtfully constructed and made possible because of the welcoming, loving atmosphere Desiree's mother created in her kitchen. The Grateful Gourmet sets out to capture even just a fraction of that essence. In doing so, Desiree, her family and the truck supply more than food; they also share an enduring tradition and passion passed down for generations.

Q&A with Owner Desiree Bagnell

Based on your truck's name, is it safe to assume you're a Grateful Dead fan?

Yes [laughs]. I'm a *huge* Grateful Dead fan, yes. In fact, I just got back from a show in Charlotte. I flew down to see them. I try to get to as many shows as I possibly can every time they're playing.

What was your first event with the truck?

The first thing was Hawk Haven Vineyard & Winery down in Cape May.

How was that experience?

Fantastic. I mean, you're a nervous wreck, because you're new and you're thinking, "All right, I've practiced with this at home. I've had it plugged in, and I *think* I know how it's going to run." But honestly, you start to work out all the kinks during that first event; your instinct kicks in, and you know how to cook and how to keep rolling. It's just the running of the register you're a little nervous with, or just being with a new team.

My husband works with us, and one of my best friends ever works alongside us, too. She usually does service. So when we have an event like that, we need to ramp up. It turned out fantastic, though after we were done that first day, we were like, "Okay, I need a glass of wine now" [laughs]. "And let's talk about what we can do better the next time."

How would you describe your menu?

I try to marry concepts from the South and also from the North. It's kind of like putting a Philly spin on certain things. Certainly I have my own little spin, but you try to keep it as classic as possible. For example, there's a pork sandwich that I do that is great; I do a barbecue pork and then throw in something really Philly, like hot cherry peppers normally on cheesesteaks.

The greatest part of this is I get to do what I feel like doing [laughs]. I have notebooks—tons of them—and I just think of crazy combinations and then test them out.

What are your most popular menu items?

Nashville Hot Chicken is one of them, for sure. Tater tots and Brussels sprouts. And you would think, "Brussels sprouts? Ew, weird." But no, I make a really funky sauce that goes on them, and people are always asking for the recipe [laughs].

Then I have some grilled cheeses that are really popular. There's one that I usually have on the menu called the Little Dreamer, and that's pretty popular. It's thick-sliced bacon with two kinds of cheese on a maple swirl bread. I also do one that's bacon jam with pears, arugula and two kinds of cheese.

What kind of catering options do you offer?

When people reach out, I send them kind of a general guideline, and I can do anything from a private dinner for two to larger parties. I like to meet my customers and get to know them or talk to them to find out what it is they're looking for. What are you trying to achieve with your event? I mean, I'm not going to be your white glove service kind of person. That makes me very nervous [laughs]. I leave that to the true chefs. So I'll go through the menu with my customers, and we try to figure out exactly what they'd like.

CHAPTER 19

MAMA DUDE'S

Thyme Honey

128 grams local honey (preferably Wilson's Honey)
10–12 sprigs thyme

Combine honey and thyme in a medium pot. Place on stove on medium heat and bring to a simmer.

As soon as it simmers, remove from heat and let sit for 10 minutes. Strain and let cool.

Store in an airtight container at room temperature.

Pepper Jam

6 large red bell peppers, deveined and quartered
2 tart apples, peeled and quartered
1 Thai chili
45 grams honey
10 grams sugar
200 grams orange juice

Place all ingredients in a medium sauce pot and cook on medium heat until liquid simmers. Then reduce to medium-low heat until liquid reduces by half.

Place into a blender and blend until smooth.

Pour into a bowl or resealable container and let cool before serving. (May be stored up to 2 weeks in the refrigerator.)

Griggstown Turkey Breakfast Tacos

Turkey Breakfast Tacos
2 tablespoons avocado oil
2 cloves garlic, diced
1 small red onion, diced
1 red pepper, diced
1 pound ground turkey (preferably from Griggstown Farm)
Salt, to taste
Pepper, to taste
Handful of arugula (local, if possible)
2 tablespoons Thyme Honey
2 eggs
3–4 flour tortillas
1 tablespoon Pepper Jam

Tzatziki Sauce (Yield: 2 cups)
3 Persian or ½ English hothouse cucumbers, cut into ¼-inch pieces
¼ cup dill
3 tablespoons olive oil
1 cup plain whole-milk Greek yogurt
2 tablespoons fresh lemon juice
1 garlic clove, lightly crushed
Kosher salt, to taste

Griggstown Turkey Breakfast Tacos: Preheat oven to 350 degrees Fahrenheit.

In a large pot, combine avocado oil, garlic, onion and pepper. Place on stove above medium-low heat and cook until translucent, roughly 5 minutes.

Once cooked, add turkey plus salt and pepper and cook on medium heat until cooked through. Once cooked, add arugula and remove from heat and cover. Let sit until arugula is wilted.

Add Thyme Honey and combine.

In a separate pan, fry two eggs on medium heat until cooked, leaving the yolk runny.

Place flour tortillas in the oven for 1 to 2 minutes, until warm but still pliable.

Tzatziki Sauce: Puree cucumber, dill and oil in food processor and combine. (A box grater will also work for the cucumber.)

Once pureed, mix in a large bowl with remaining ingredients and season to taste.

Assemble: To assemble, place tortillas down followed by Pepper Jam and turkey mixture. Then place fried eggs on top and enjoy.

Tip: These tacos pair nicely with CAP•SAI•CIN Magma Powder or any preferred hot sauce.

Pickled Grapes

2 bunches cotton candy grapes
90 percent apple cider vinegar
5 percent neutral oil
5 percent water
30 grams honey
2 grams salt
2 grams pepper

Wash grapes and cut in half. Place into a medium sauce pot. Then cover three-quarters of the way with apple cider vinegar. Add remaining ingredients.

Place on high flame and cook until rolling boil starts. Then remove from heat and strain.

Allow grapes to cool by spreading on a baking sheet.

Store in airtight container. (May be stored up to 5 days in the refrigerator.)

꙳

WASTE NOT, WANT NOT

New Jersey boasts more than 700,000 acres of farmland divided between nearly ten thousand farms. As a result, the state is a leading producer of many fruits and vegetables, including blueberries, cranberries, peaches, bell peppers and spinach. Many farms also grow apples, corn, hay, potatoes, soybeans, strawberries, tomatoes and more. To celebrate the wealth of high-quality produce New Jersey has to offer, the Mama Dude's food truck bases their menu on delicious produce from local farmers.

Mama Dude's owner chef Andrew Dudich is a lifelong Mercer County resident. He grew up in Hamilton Township, attending Mercer County Vo-Tech's culinary program in high school. After graduation, Andrew enrolled at Johnson & Wales University in Providence, Rhode Island, further expanding his culinary education.

During Andrew's senior year of college, his mother passed away. This was especially difficult because she was a major inspiration behind his interest in cooking. In fact, her alma mater was Johnson & Wales, and she was the cook at home. "Her rule of thumb was if you're walking through the kitchen, you better be ready to help cook," Andrew recalls.

Following in her footsteps, Andrew became enthralled by cuisine. He studied and practiced numerous styles, developing his own precise methods and skills. His original aim was to work at fine-dining restaurants in Boston and New York.

After his mother's passing, Andrew finished college and returned home to spend time with his younger brother and rethink his future. First, he started a catering business called the Spring Chicken, which he maintained full time for several months. Then one day, he saw a food truck for sale in someone's driveway, and right away he knew what he wanted to do.

A DASH OF MAMA, A PINCH OF DUDICH

Andrew immediately bought the truck and built it out to fit his needs. He got a Trenton artist to design and paint the exterior and spent some time planning his concept. He named his truck Mama Dude's, paying homage to

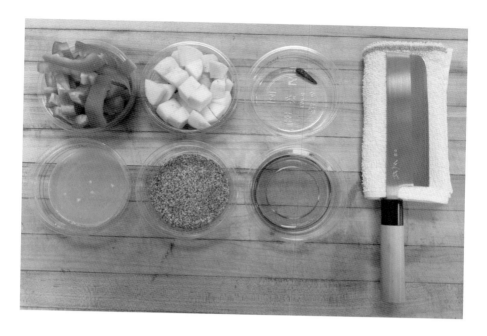

his late mother. As for the concept, Mama Dude's sources all produce from New Jersey farms. In particular, Andrew works with five different farmers to acquire whatever is in season. He specifically uses any produce they have too much of and integrates it into his menu. Therefore, the menu changes four times a year. But as long as an item or ingredient is in season, Andrew says it'll likely return to the menu the following year.

The menu is simple and organized. When guests order from Mama Dude's, they choose a base, protein, topping and sauce. Base options include local greens, jasmine rice or half and half, while proteins range from meats like pork, beef and chicken to vegetables such as squash, avocado, cauliflower and even ratatouille. Patrons then select one or more toppings from a list of cucumbers, cheeses, asparagus, cured egg yolk, mozzarella in basil oil and more. Of course, the available choices depend on the season. However, Andrew keeps a steady selection of sauces.

When the truck first pressed the pavement, it was one of the only farm-to-table trucks in New Jersey. But despite their unique offerings, Mama Dude's was unable to take off at many events in its debut season. However, the truck found a huge following at different farmers' markets throughout the state and also served as a successful catering option.

The Future of Mama Dude's

After several years with the truck, Andrew decided to grow his business. In early 2020, he found an old deli available to rent in his hometown. He signed the lease the day before the state shut down due to the COVID-19 pandemic, which prevented the Mama Dude's brick-and-mortar from opening until the end of that year. Once the doors did open, the storefront gained its own following of devoted guests. First, the people who frequented the truck at markets and events became regulars, and then Andrew started seeing new faces in his shop.

For his storefront, Andrew adopts a fast-casual restaurant style, but it's a little closer to upscale dining with quick service. The menu is reminiscent of the truck's but expands to offer exclusive items like a fried peanut butter and jelly sandwich or the pork roll, egg and fontina cheese sandwich using homemade biscuits as bread.

Mama Dude's makes everything in-house, sourcing local ingredients to create dishes patrons can't find at many other places in the state. Andrew takes pride in his food, but more than that, Mama Dude's is a testament to his mother, whose inspiration, imprint and legacy live on through his success as a chef and a food trucker.

Q&A with Owner Andrew Dudich

Did you ever want to open your own restaurant?
No, the plan was to work for someone who knew a lot more than I did at the time. I know how to cook, but what you see out of those chefs are the foams and the powders and the molecular gastronomy. All the cool stuff you see on the Food Network and *Chopped*. That's probably where I would've ended up. I had plans of going to England and cooking there and traveling. The plans changed a lot, but everything happens for a reason.

How does your truck menu differ from your restaurant's menu?
I'll reach out to four, five farms we're close with, ask them what they're using, what they have too much of, and that's how we'll make our menus. What's in season goes on the menu. For example, I texted my farmer the other day and asked him what he had. He said, "I got a ton of beets," so we'll probably be

putting beets on the menu. He has a ton of parsnips, so those are going to go on. We make everything in house, from sauces to toppings. That's why we don't put "house made" on anything, because it's all house made.

Do any of your popular items ever come back to the menu?

If it's in season, yeah [laughs]. A good example is in the winter we have burnt carrots. It's not like we're doing anything crazy back here. It's honest cooking, clean. Those'll be back, because carrots will be back in season. Stuff like that, if it's a fan favorite, it'll absolutely come back. But I like to change things up and get creative if I can.

What is it like now owning a business in the town you grew up in?

That's a good question [laughs]. It definitely helped in the beginning. We opened in December 2020, which, if you remember, was like mid-pandemic. We had a lot of support from friends and family. As much as I'd like to think the food's exceptional, I think every restaurant needs that boost right off the bat to get through. We're doing fine now, and I see less of the family and friends, which is just what you want.

What were some of your experiences opening up your restaurant during a pandemic?

The original plan was to open in May, but we weren't even close to that. Right before then, there was the construction ban, so we couldn't even get in the store until June, and then we had to gut the whole store because this used to be an old deli. So this is all new walls, floors, plumbing—it's a brand-new store. Then getting equipment in was tough. We ordered our equipment in August; it didn't come until the end of October. That was probably the biggest problem trying to open during the pandemic.

CHAPTER 20

SURF AND TURF TRUCK

BLT Lobster Roll

¼ ounce butter, and additional butter (per preference)
Split-top white hoagie roll
2 ounces organic greens
4 ounces knuckle and claw lobster meat
2 ounces bacon, chopped
1 ounce sun-dried tomato, diced
1 drizzle white truffle oil

Butter the split-top roll and toast it in a pan over medium heat or in a toaster oven.

Remove roll from heat and pack with greens.

Take the lobster meat and place in pan on low to medium heat. Put as much butter as you'd like in the pan with the lobster meat.

Once cooked and heated thoroughly, remove lobster meat from pan and place it in the roll.

Cook a slice of bacon to your desired crispiness. Chop into fine pieces and place on top of the lobster meat.

Dice sun-dried tomato. Garnish lobster roll with sun-dried tomato and a drizzle of white truffle oil.

Enjoy!

~~~

COAST TO COAST

When Cindy Matas tore open her acceptance letter for California State University–Long Beach, she never intended to be brought back to her home state as a food trucker just ten years later.

Cindy was born and raised in Hamilton Township, Mercer County. After high school, she moved out to California, earning a bachelor's degree in American studies. For nearly a decade, she worked out in the Golden State, holding several positions with Sony Corporation. She started with Sony Connect and then moved over to the PlayStation division before working in the eBook division. When Sony announced that they were relocating her office from Los Angeles to San Jose, Cindy considered a career change. She even toyed with the idea of moving back home. She loved the West Coast, but she was ready to return to her roots to settle down.

At that same time, Cindy's sister and brother-in-law—Beata and Adam Browne—were developing a concept for a food truck. Surf and Turf Truck, they were going to call it. Simple, familiar and unforgettable. They planned to offer a selection of shellfish and hearty meats. They enjoyed cooking and loved to eat—so a business revolving around food was a no-brainer. Cindy immediately moved back to her hometown and became a founding member of Surf and Turf Truck in 2013.

Riding the Wave

The Surf and Turf Truck brand centers on the laid-back, spirited vibes of beach life. With a fresh set of wheels, Cindy, Beata and Adam sought to bring these vibes to residents across New Jersey and eastern Pennsylvania. The group utilized their skills from the corporate world to forge their business, but they needed the industry know-how to really get those wheels turning without slowing down.

Their first time out with the truck was for a lunch service in Philadelphia. Even before they opened the window, the trio was prepared for nothing short of chaos. Cindy, Beata and Adam took the process one step at a time— one *event* at a time—sincerely grading themselves after each outing. Soon enough, Surf and Turf Truck was locked into a groove. They were regularly attending events throughout the tristate area, taking on catering gigs and trying their luck curbside in various cities.

Not long after, the truck was featured on Travel Channel's show *Food Paradise*, in the aptly titled "Surf and Turf" episode. They also appeared on the Cooking Channel and ABC's *FYI Philly*. It helped cement Surf and Turf Truck's reputation in the local food truck scenes.

A Memorable Menu

Adam developed Surf and Turf Truck's menu. After years of working in the Hamptons and vacationing in Maine, he had the idea to bring those famous lobster rolls to both the Garden State and the City of Brotherly Love.

Arguably, Surf and Turf couldn't live up to its name if it didn't fluidly combine both styles of cuisine into one robust sandwich. The Surf and Turf Sandwich (a secret menu item) combines the warm lobster roll and the Rosemary Steak Sandwich. This behemoth of a hoagie actually overflows with lobster and beef, and hardcore Surf and Turf Truck followers never miss an opportunity to order it when they spot the vibrant red-and-green logo at festivals and events.

During the summer of 2015, Cindy took over complete operations of the lone Surf and Turf Truck in the Northeast. Beata and Adam moved down to Florida, graciously handing the reins over to their sister. Enlisting the help of her close friends, Cindy and her crew spent a couple years managing a restaurant in Peddler's Village in Lahaska, Pennsylvania, while also operating the truck on the side. Eventually, Cindy decided to focus her attention solely on the truck, catering celebrations, attending events and providing lunch and dinner services all around the area.

Q&A WITH CO-FOUNDER/OWNER CINDY MATAS

What year and where did you start Surf and Turf Truck?

In 2013, Surf and Turf Truck was born in Hamilton, New Jersey. I was trying to decide what direction to go with my career. Moving back to the East Coast to be closer to family and start a new venture in the burgeoning food truck industry sounded like a great adventure! So, I packed up my bags, said goodbye to the City of Angels and headed back to good old New Jersey.

What was that transition like, moving back to New Jersey after being in California?

It's funny because people always say the joke that "you always come back east after living out west." For me, it was the right choice to come back home after living away for over a decade to be closer to family and start my new career. You can always come home again; just be ready for actual weather again [laughs].

What were those first few years with the food truck like?

The first years were super exciting, nerve-racking and overall chaos in the beginning! We took each day and grew from it. We had to learn what systems to put in place to operate efficiently. Trial and error were our best friends! Once we started getting everything in order and what events to do, it really became such an awesome time. The food truck industry is its own little subculture, and you really do become friends with so many vendors along the way.

Everyone helps each other out when in need, which really creates lasting bonds. It sounds cheesy, but it's totally true! Many trucks have come and gone, but it's nice to stay in touch with people who understand all the crazy ups and downs of "food truck life."

Tell us about your menu.

We serve three styles of lobster rolls: a Warm Lobster Roll, a BLT Lobster Roll and a Chilled Lobster Roll. We also serve a Rosemary Steak Sandwich topped with just buttered lobster. We also do Shrimp Tacos, a Shrimp Po' Boy and even two vegan options. We do a vegan garlic truffle aioli on our Veggie Burger and a Spicy Tofu Sandwich. People really love that we have such a nice variety of menu items. We really have something for everyone!

How much has Surf and Turf Truck evolved over the years?

Some days and events were fantastic! Things would go smooth; it's beautiful weather, and everyone in the crowd is in a great mood. Then there are other days where it starts pouring rain or the truck breaks down on the way to an event. This business can try your patience and sanity for sure, just like any business. You just have to want it and—totally corny but—"keep on truckin'!" Over the years, we have learned what works for us event-wise and have stayed true to our original menu. We've featured other items— the Lobster Grilled Cheese, Bacon-Onion Burger—but have always kept our "signature menu," if you will. But it's always fun to try different items, especially with a name like Surf and Turf.

What can you tell us about your menu?

We offer good, quality food that is made with LOVE! Our menu is focused on simple, delicious eats you would have if you were hanging out at the beach or poolside. That's our motto: "we bring the beach to you, curbside!" We truly do enjoy bringing the laid-back, beach vibes to all our customers.

Do you have any advice for those who want to get into the food trucking industry?

You must be the right mix of insane and stable to handle this industry. Make sure you have your systems in place, and then you'll be golden. You also better love long drives! [Laughs]

ABOUT THE AUTHORS

PATRICK LOMBARDI is a lifelong New Jersey resident. He graduated from Rider University in Lawrenceville, New Jersey, with a bachelor's degree in English. He is a full-time employee with the state and contributes original content to Best of NJ (bestofnj.com). He has been published in outlets such as *BuzzFeed*, NJ.com, *Odyssey*, MyCentralJersey.com and Patch.com. His first book, *Junk Sale*, a collection of humorous short stories and essays, was published in August 2018. To see his latest projects, visit his website at www.patricklombardi.com. Follow him on Instagram/Twitter @patlombardi4 or on Facebook @PatrickLombardiWriter.

VINCENT PARISI is the editor-in-chief for Best of NJ (bestofnj.com). He is a New Jersey native, born and raised in Bergen County, with a bachelor's degree in journalism from Ramapo College of New Jersey. Prior to his current position, Vincent spent years as a journalist in the video game industry, writing for outlets such as *Scholar Gamers* and *IGX Pro*, before becoming editor-in-chief of *IndieGameMagazine*. After years of covering the video game space, he

pivoted to more general content, arriving at Best of NJ as a writer to cover local events.

By his second year, Vincent became editor-in-chief, in charge of content production, web design and many other facets of the rapidly growing online outlet. As the leader of Best of NJ, Vincent's goal is to spotlight both popular and brand-new local businesses, helping business owners reach a wide audience while also becoming the go-to source for readers looking to find the best places to eat, upcoming events and top-quality services in their area.

During his tenure as editor-in-chief, Vincent has developed a number of original series with his writing team, from "The Best New Jersey Hiking Trails" to "I HeART New Jersey" (a series that showcases talented local artists and makers), as well as "Jersey Through History" (written and photographic tours of the state's most historic sites and landmarks) and "The Best New Jersey Food Trucks," the inspiration for this very book. Beyond original series, Best of NJ is famous for the website's "Best of" lists, ranking as the number-one search result on Google for their mega-popular features such as "The Best Outdoor Dining Restaurants in New Jersey," "The Best Brunch Spots in New Jersey," "The Best Full-Service Hair Salons in New Jersey" and many, many more. From spas to s'mores, he has worked with all types of New Jersey businesses, both big and small, and thoroughly enjoys telling the stories of their owners.

Vincent loves helping local businesses grow and develop their online presence and connecting with Best of NJ readers about what businesses the outlet should feature next. He hopes to continue developing new ways to feature New Jersey's incredible restaurants, services, venues and more and is determined to make Best of NJ the most popular website in the state for local business recommendations, original editorials, event calendars and more. Follow him on Twitter @Vincent_Parisi.